Kalamazoo County and the Civil War

Gary L. Gibson

Published by The History Press
Charleston, SC
www.historypress.com

Copyright © 2021 by Gary L. Gibson
All rights reserved

First published 2021

Manufactured in the United States

ISBN 9781467145855

Library of Congress Control Number: 2020945883

Notice: The information in this book is true and complete to the best of our knowledge. It is offered without guarantee on the part of the author or The History Press. The author and The History Press disclaim all liability in connection with the use of this book.

All rights reserved. No part of this book may be reproduced or transmitted in any form whatsoever without prior written permission from the publisher except in the case of brief quotations embodied in critical articles and reviews.

Contents

Preface	5
Acknowledgements	7
1. A Time of Growth	9
2. Abraham Lincoln's Visit to Kalamazoo	14
3. The War Comes to Kalamazoo County	23
4. Kalamazoo Prepares for War	28
5. The Black Community	52
6. The Homefront	61
7. The War Ends	70
8. The Postwar Years	76
9. Stories of the Veterans	113
Epilogue	139
Appendix	141
Bibliography	153
Index	169
About the Author	175

Preface

There have been several thousands of books written about the Civil War. Thousands of books about the battles, the generals and Abraham Lincoln have been published. Unfortunately, there have not been very many books about what went on in the small, close-knit communities of the Midwest. How did the people react and respond when the news of the Southern states seceding from the Union arrived over the telegraph wires?

This book relates the other side of the Civil War story. When news came to Kalamazoo County about the surrender of Fort Sumter, the citizens' reaction was one of determination. As most Michiganders would, they put their minds and backs to the task. The Union must be preserved.

During my research, I was disappointed to learn that there is very little in the way of letters and diaries kept by county residents that are accessible, and within those that are, not much is written in reaction to the events occurring outside of southwestern Michigan.

One collection of letters, located in the archives of Western Michigan University, is from the Hodgman family of Climax, Michigan, in southeastern Kalamazoo County. Moses Hodgman was a shoe and boot maker, earning a decent living and supporting his family. He was able to send one son, Frank, to the state college in Lansing, now Michigan State University. Moses's eldest son, Samuel, enlisted in Company I, 7th Michigan Infantry as a sergeant on June 28, 1861. He was thirty years of age. The 7th was encamped and trained at Fort Wayne, situated on the Detroit River. Before leaving Michigan for the front, Sam came home to visit his family. When Sam's short leave was over,

Preface

he headed back to Detroit. Moses, in a letter to Frank on August 25, told him, "It would have made your heart ache to see Sam start from here alone on foot with his soldier's pack alike for the cause and the effect. He has given himself to his country and may God in his infinite mercy bless, protect and guide him in safety through every toil."

Sometimes we forget the human side of great events. We live our lives on a day-to-day basis, influenced to some degree by outside forces—those incidents and people outside of our own little world. Occasionally, no matter what we do to block them out, the events take precedent and we have to adjust our own world to the times in which we live. The World War II generation had to do this. While writing this in 2020, we are doing this with the COVID-19 virus pandemic. It was the same with the Civil War generation.

I hope that this volume will tell the story of our citizens of Kalamazoo County who came before us and that their experiences will inspire present and future residents of the county of the Boiling Waters.

Acknowledgements

An undertaking such as this would be impossible without the assistance and support of several individuals. I am fortunate to count them all as friends and colleagues:

Dr. Sharon Carlson, Regional History Collections director; John Winchell, Archives curator; and Lynn Houghton, Regional History Collections curator, Zhang Legacy and Collections Center, Archives and Regional History Collections, Western Michigan University.

Regina Gorham, collections manager, Kalamazoo Valley Museum.

Matt VanAcker, Capital Education director and Save the Flags co-chair, State Capital Commission, and Cambray Sampson, curator, Save the Flags, Lansing, Michigan.

Steve Rossio, city historian, Portage District Library, and past commander, General Benjamin Pritchard Camp No. 20, Sons of Union Veterans of the Civil War.

Keith G. Harrison, board president, Michigan's Grand Army of the Republic Memorial Hall and Museum, Eaton Rapids, Michigan, and past commander-in-chief, Sons of Union Veterans of the Civil War.

Robert Hencken and Don Jarzambek, Kalamazoo Detachment No. 879, Marine Corps League, Kalamazoo.

Dr. Tom George, former state senator and board member, Kalamazoo Abraham Lincoln Project.

Gary L. Swain, board member, Kalamazoo Abraham Lincoln Project, and past commander, General Benjamin Pritchard Camp No. 20, Sons of Union Veterans of the Civil War.

Acknowledgements

Michael B. Culp, executive director, 13th Michigan Memorial Association, and past commander, General Benjamin Pritchard Camp No. 20, Sons of Union Veterans of the Civil War, and Marianne Lancaster, secretary, 13th Michigan Memorial Association.

My editor, John Rodrigue of The History Press, whose patience and guidance through this process is greatly appreciated.

I must also include my wife and best friend, Beth, whose unwavering support of my zealous involvement in several organizations and projects means a great deal.

1
A Time of Growth

Kalamazoo in the Antebellum Period

Kalamazoo County, Michigan, was organized on July 30, 1830, when Saint Joseph County was subdivided into six counties: Saint Joseph, Kalamazoo, Calhoun, Branch, Barry and Eaton. Along the banks of the Kalamazoo River and Arcadia Creek, a vigorous community, originally called Bronson, flourished in the rough country. The land office in present-day Schoolcraft was busy working with new settlers with dreams of newfound prosperity. The small Greek Revival building still stands and is currently the barber shop on the east side of US 131 in the center of the village.

The twenty-four years since statehood in 1837 saw a period of growth that included not only agriculture but also several manufacturing enterprises that continued the expansion. In 1848, the State of Michigan selected Kalamazoo County as the location to establish the Michigan Asylum for the Insane on what is now Oakland Drive at the present site of the Western Michigan University School of Nursing. The introduction of the railroad, from Detroit to Kalamazoo, made travel through southern Michigan easy by the day's standards. The population of the county swelled to 24,746 in 1860. The village of Kalamazoo boasted 6,945 residents, both White and Black.

Kalamazoo County sent 3,321 soldiers to the service of the United States during the Civil War. Of those, 396 did not return; their names are inscribed on a plaque in Veteran's Memorial Hall in the county courthouse.

Main Street (Michigan Avenue) in Kalamazoo, circa 1870. *Kalamazoo Valley Museum Collection.*

Most were farm boys from around the village of Kalamazoo and the other small villages and crossroads in the area—Carpenter's Corners (at the intersection of South Westnedge Avenue and Milham Road), Portage Center, Galesburg, Vicksburg, Schoolcraft, Fulton, Cooper, Alamo, Yorkville, Climax and Scotts. Many had never been outside of Kalamazoo County and very few, if any, outside of the state of Michigan. Many now lie in graves in places far from home.

During the war, Michigan raised thirty-one regiments of infantry, eleven regiments of cavalry, one regiment of light artillery, one regiment of engineers and mechanics and one regiment of sharpshooters. One of those regiments of infantry, the 6th Michigan, would be reorganized and retrained as heavy artillery. Unique to Michigan was that instead of creating new regiments as the earlier units became depleted in numbers, like Indiana or Pennsylvania, which had upward of three hundred regiments, Michigan simply added men to the regiments it had in the field. Over eighty-eight thousand men (and one well-documented woman) served in the Union forces from Michigan. The regiments were in all of the bloodiest and most crucial battles of the war, and they returned to the state with impeccable records.

A major part of Kalamazoo's contribution to the cause was providing a place for several regiments to rendezvous, train and prepare for what was to come. Eventually, there would be six regiments of infantry, one company of sharpshooters and one artillery battery that encamped and trained in Kalamazoo at the National Race Track, a renowned horse racing establishment that was located in the current Washington Square neighborhood in the southern part of the city.

From a hillside trading post within what are now the boundaries of Riverside Cemetery, to a thriving community, Kalamazoo County was to play its part in the upheaval that was unfolding on the American landscape.

THE ROAD TO FREEDOM

Dr. Nathan M. Thomas was the first physician to settle in Kalamazoo County. Born at Mount Pleasant, Ohio, in 1803, he migrated to Michigan in 1833 and chose the grasslands of Prairie Rhonde for his home, now part of Schoolcraft. The doctor built his small Greek Revival–style home in 1835 at Cass and Center Streets and practiced medicine there. Dr. Thomas married Pamela S. Brown of Vermont in 1840. After taking his bride, he added two wings to the house, enlarging it to its present-day size. He also owned a farm north of the village of Vicksburg. Nathan Thomas was a religious man and was a member of the Society of Friends, commonly referred to as Quakers.

As a Quaker, Dr. Thomas was adamantly opposed to slavery; the aversion to it was instilled in him from an early age. Mrs. Thomas would remember many years later that she "thought him fanatical" when her husband stated, "Slavery cannot continue to exist under our Government. If it is not put down by the ballot, it will go down in blood."

Even before his marriage, Dr. Thomas had a reputation for his willingness to assist runaway slaves. The doctor was, at that time, residing at the hotel in Schoolcraft, and many of those fleeing bondage sought out his aid and protection. As a married couple, the Thomases worked as a team in their illegal venture. Mrs. Thomas's recollections included this account:

> *After we began housekeeping they came singly and by twos and threes. The first was a woman, advanced in years, who had made her way on foot and alone from Missouri, at first helped by people of her own color, then by Friends* [Quakers], *who were always ready to aid the fleeing slaves. This woman was an eloquent talker. She told me of what some of the women had to endure from cruel licentious masters. From that time I felt it was my duty to do the little I could for those attempting to escape from bondage.*

About 1843, the Thomas house became an official stop on the Underground Railroad. The Thomases would transport the slaves, give them a place to rest and feed them. Zachariah Shutgart of Cass County and Erastus Hussey of Battle Creek, both Quakers, organized the route to be taken across southern Michigan. After the delivery of the "cargo" from Mr. Shutgart, Dr. Thomas was to convey the former slaves through Vicksburg

Dr. Nathan Thomas House, Schoolcraft. The house is now a museum owned by the Schoolcraft Historical Society. *Photo by the author.*

A Time of Growth

to Climax and then on to Mr. Hussey. This round trip took all night or, on occasion, all day in broad daylight. From Battle Creek, the fugitives would go to Marshall and then on to Ann Arbor and finally to Detroit, where they would be ferried across the river and into Canada and, finally, to freedom. Aside from his work assisting runaways, Thomas maintained his medical practice, keeping his secret from his patients.

As slave catchers were known to come as far north as southern Michigan, the Thomases had to be very careful. Dr. and Mrs. Thomas risked being imprisoned for their efforts, due to the Fugitive Slave Act of 1850. The law provided that slave owners could enter the northern free states, hunt down the escapees and return them to bondage. Slave catchers served the same purpose as what one might call a bounty hunter today.

By the end of the Civil War, the Thomases estimated that they had assisted between 1,000 and 1,500 runaway slaves. Nathan and Pamela also had four children during those years. In 1868, Dr. Thomas moved the old house to its present location at 613 East Cass Street and built a new brick house on the site of the old house. That house also still stands.

In her autobiography, Pamela Thomas wrote, "It is now thirty to forty years since the last of the long train of fugitives stopped at our house on the road to freedom, and I, an old lady of seventy-six years, feel glad and proud of my small share in the glorious emancipation consummated by our martyr president in his proclamation of 1863."

Dr. Nathan Thomas died in Schoolcraft on April 7, 1887, at the age of eighty-four. His beloved wife, Pamela, died on January 27, 1909, at the age of ninety-two. Both are buried at the Schoolcraft Cemetery.

2

Abraham Lincoln's Visit to Kalamazoo

In 1856, John C. Frémont was an aspirant for president of the United States—the first candidate from the newly minted Republican Party. Hezekiah G. Wells, a staunch supporter of the new party's ideals, was serving as a judge in the village of Kalamazoo. Judge Wells had heard of a forty-seven-year-old lawyer from Illinois who had made a name for himself running for a seat as a United States senator the year before. If Wells could persuade him to come to Kalamazoo and speak, it would be a boost to the party, even if the speaker had lost to his opponent. The speaker was Abraham Lincoln.

Wells wrote to Lincoln on July 24, 1856, asking him to attend the Freemont Mass Meeting on August 27, in Bronson Park. Lincoln responded in a letter dated August 4, stating:

> *It would afford me great pleasure to be with you, and will do so if possible, but I can not promise positively. We are having trouble here that needs the attention of all of us—I mean the Fillmore movement. With the Freemont and Fillmore men united, here in Illinois, we have Mr. Buchanan in the hollow of our hand—but with us divided, as we are now, he has us. This is the short and simple truth, as I believe.*
> *Very Respectfully,*
> *A. Lincoln*

Abraham Lincoln's Visit to Kalamazoo

The letter gives the impression that Lincoln might not have ever come to Michigan, let alone Kalamazoo. The trouble with the Fillmore movement in Illinois must have been resolved in time. This letter is currently in the collection of the Kalamazoo Valley Museum. It seems that there are a few differences of opinion about some of the aspects of Lincoln's visit, one of which is where he stayed while in Kalamazoo. The more prevalent argument is that Wells hosted Lincoln in his home, located on the southwest corner of Park Street and South Street, where the Kalamazoo Institute of Arts now stands. It would afford Lincoln a very short walk to Bronson Park. A Kalamazoo resident's written reminiscence states, however, that Lincoln stayed at the Burdick House Hotel on the north side of Main Street, between Rose and Burdick Streets. The account asserts, "He had arrived that morning from Chicago, and when the committee went to the Burdick House and rapped at his room they were bid to 'come in,' in a most hearty fashion, and on entering beheld a tall, sallow, black haired man, with his face covered with lather and a razor in his hand. It was Mr. Lincoln shaving himself. It will be remembered that he never let his beard grow until after he was president."

On August 27, 1856, in Bronson Park, there were several speakers on four different platforms that had been erected for the event. That morning, Lincoln would walk the short distance from his lodgings to the green space. This would be Lincoln's only public appearance and speech in Michigan. From various accounts, there were several thousand people in Kalamazoo for the rally. Kalamazoo resident George Washington Winslow, a headstone maker who was present at Jackson, Michigan, when the Republican Party was born "under the oaks," enthusiastically introduced the lanky, six-foot-four-inch man from the Prairie State. Lincoln's speech followed:

> *Fellow countrymen:*
> *Under the Constitution of the United States another Presidential contest approaches us. All over this land—that portion, at least, of which I know much—the people are assembling to consider the proper course to be adopted by them. One of the first considerations is to learn what the people differ about. If we ascertain what we differ about, we shall be better able to decide.*
>
> *The question of slavery, at the present day, should not only be the greatest question, but very nearly the sole question. Our opponents, however, prefer that this should not be the case. To get at this question, I will occupy your attention but a single moment.*

The question is simply this: Shall slavery be into new territories, or not? This is the naked question. If we should support Fremont successfully in this, it may be charged that we will not be content with restricting slavery in the new territories. If we should charge that James Buchanan, by his platform, is bound to extend slavery into the territories, and that he is in favor of its being thus spread, we should be puzzled to prove it. We believe it, nevertheless.

By taking the issue as I present it, whether it shall be permitted as an issue, is made up between the parties. Each takes his own stand. This is the question: Shall the Government of the United States prohibit slavery in the [territories of the] *United States?*

We have been in the habit of deploring the fact that slavery exists among us. We have ever deplored it. Our forefathers did, and they declared, as we have done in later years, the blame rested upon the mother government of Great Britain. We constantly condemn Great Britain for not preventing slavery from coming amongst us. She would not interfere to prevent it, and so individuals were able to introduce the institution without opposition. I have alluded to this, to ask you if this is not exactly the policy of Buchanan and his friends, to place this government in the attitude then occupied by the government of Great Britain—placing the nation in the position to authorize the territories to reproach it, for refusing to allow them to hold slaves.

I would like to ask your attention, any gentlemen to tell me when the people of Kansas are going to decide. When are they to do it? I asked that question two years ago—when, and how are [they] *to do it? Not many weeks ago, our new Senator from Illinois* [Mr. Trumbull], *asked Douglas how it could be done. Douglas is a great man – at keeping from answering questions he don't want to answer. He would not answer. He said it was a question for the Supreme Court to decide. In the North, his friends argue that the people can decide at any time.*

The Southerners say there is no power in the people, whatever. We know that from the time white people have been allowed in the territory they have brought slaves with them. Suppose the people come up to vote as freely, and with as perfect protection as we could do it here. Will they be at liberty to vote their sentiments? If they can, then all that has ever been said about our provincial ancestors is untrue, and they could have done so, also. We know our Southern friends say that the General Government cannot interfere. They could as truly say, "It is amongst us—we cannot get rid of it."

But I am afraid I waste too much time on this point. I take it as an illustration of the principle, that slaves are admitted to the territories. And, while I am speaking of Kansas, how will that operate? Can men vote truly? We will suppose that there are ten men who go into Kansas to settle. Nine of these are opposed to slavery. One has ten slaves. The slaveholder is a good man in other respects; he is a good neighbor, and being a wealthy man, he is enabled to do the others many neighborly kindnesses. They like the man, although they don't like the system by which he holds his fellowmen in bondage. And here, let me say, that in intellectual and physical structure, our Southern brethren do not differ from us. They are, like us, subject to passions, and it is only their odious institution of slavery, that makes the breach between us.

These ten men of whom I was speaking, live together three or four years; they intermarry; their family ties are strengthened. And who wonders that in time, the people learn to look upon slavery with complacency? This is the way in which slavery is planted, and gains so firm a foothold. I think this is a strong card that the Nebraska party have played, and won upon, in this game.

I suppose that this crowd are opposed to the admission of slavery into Kansas, yet it is true that in all crowds there are some who differ from the majority. I want to ask the Buchanan men, who are against the spread of slavery, if there be any present, why not vote for the man who is against it? I understand that Mr. Fillmore's position is precisely like Buchanan's. I understand that, by the Nebraska bill, a door has been opened for the spread of slavery in the territories. Examine, if you please, and see if they have ever done any such thing as try to shut the door.

It is true that Fillmore tickles a few of his friends with the notion that he is not the cause of the door being opened. Well; it brings him into this position: he tries to get both sides, one by denouncing those who opened the door, and the other by hinting that he doesn't care a fig for its being open. If he were President, he would have one side or the other—he would either restrict slavery or not. Of course it would be so. There could be no middle way.

You who hate slavery and love freedom, why not, as Fillmore and Buchanan are on the same ground, vote for Fremont? Why not vote for the man who takes your side of the question? "Well," says Buchanan, "it is none of our business." But is it not our business? There are several reasons why I think it is our business. But let us see how it is. Others have urged these reasons before, but they are still of use. By our Constitution we are represented in Congress in proportion to our numbers, and in counting the numbers that give us our representatives, three slaves are counted as 2 people. The State of Maine has six representatives in the lower house of Congress. In strength South Carolina is equal to her. But stop! Maine has twice as many white people, and 32,000 to boot! And is that fair? I don't complain of it. This regulation was put in force when the exigencies of the times demanded it, and could not have been avoided. Now, one man in South Carolina is the same as two men here.

Maine should have twice as many men in Congress as South Carolina. It is a fact that any man in South Carolina has more influence and power in Congress today than any two now before me. The same thing is true of all slave States, though it may not be in the same proportion. It is a truth that cannot be denied, that in all the free States no white man is the equal of the white man of the slave States. But this is in the Constitution, and we must stand up to it. The question, then, is, "Have we no interest as to whether the white man of the North shall be the equal of the white man of the South?"

Once when I used this argument in the presence of Douglas, he answered that in the North the black man was counted as a full man, and had an equal vote with the white, while at the South they were counted at but three-fifths. And Douglas, when he had made this reply, doubtless thought he had forever silenced the objection.

Have we no interest in the free Territories of the United States—that they should be kept open for the homes of free white people? As our Northern States are growing more and more in wealth and population, we are continually in want of an outlet, through which it may pass out to enrich our country. In this we have an interest—a deep and abiding interest. There is another thing, and that is the mature knowledge we have—the greatest interest of all. It is the doctrine, that the people are driven from the maxims of our free Government, that despises the spirit which for eighty years has celebrated the anniversary of our national independence.

We are a great empire. We are eighty years old. We stand at once the wonder and admiration of the whole world, and we must enquire [sic] what it is that has given us so much prosperity, and we shall understand that to give up that one thing, would be to give up all future prosperity. This cause is that every man can make himself. It has been said that such a race of prosperity has been run nowhere else. We find a people on the Northeast, who have a different government from ours, being ruled by a Queen. Turning to the South, we see a people who, while they boast of being free, keep their fellow beings in bondage. Compare our Free States with either, shall we say here that we have no interest in keeping that principle alive? Shall we say,

Abraham Lincoln's Visit to Kalamazoo

"Let it be"? No—we have an interest in the maintenance of the principles of the Government, and without this interest, it is worth nothing.

I have noticed in Southern newspapers, particularly the Richmond Enquirer, *the Southern view of the Free States. They insist that slavery has a right to spread. They defend it on principle. They insist that their slaves are far better off than Northern freemen. What a mistaken view do these men have of Northern laborers! They think that men are always to remain laborers here—but there is no such class. The man who labored for another last year, this year labors for himself, and next year he will hire others to labor for him. These men don't understand when they think in this manner of Northern free labor. When these reasons can be introduced, tell me not that we have no interest in keeping the territories free for the settlement of free laborers.*

I pass, then, from this question. I think we have an ever growing interest in maintaining the free institutions of our country.

It is said that our party is a sectional party. It has been said in high quarters that if Fremont and Dayton were elected the Union would be dissolved. I believe it, that the South does so think! I believe it! It is a shameful thing that the subject is talked of so much. Did we not have a Southern President and Vice-President at one time? And yet the Union has not been dissolved. Why, at this very moment, there is a Northern President and Vice-President. Pierce and King were elected, and King died without ever taking his seat. The Senate elected a Northern man from their own numbers, to perform the duties of the Vice-President. He resigned his seat, however, as soon as he got the job of making a slave State out of Kansas. Was not that a great mistake?

(A voice: "He didn't mean that!")

Then why didn't he speak what he did mean? Why did he not speak what he ought to have spoken? That was the very thing. He should have spoken manly, and we should then have known where to have found him. It is said we expect to elect Fremont by Northern votes. Certainly we do not think the South will elect him. But let us ask the question differently. Does not Buchanan expect to be elected by Southern votes? Fillmore, however, will go out of this contest the most national man we have. He has no prospect of having a single vote on either side of Mason and Dixon's line, to trouble his poor soul about.

(Laughter and cheers)

We believe it is right that slavery should not be tolerated in the new territories, yet we cannot get support for this doctrine, except in one part of the country. Slavery is looked upon by men in the light of dollars and cents. The estimated worth of the slaves at the South is $1,000,000,000, and in a very few years if the institution shall be admitted into the new territories, they will have increased fifty percent in value.

Our adversaries charge Fremont with being an abolitionist. When pressed to show proof, they frankly confess that they can show no such thing. They run off upon the assertion that his supporters are abolitionists. But this they have never attempted to prove. I know of no word in the language that has been used so much as that one, "abolitionist," having no definition. It has no meaning unless taken as designated as a person who is abolishing something. If that be its signification, the supporters of Fremont are not abolitionists.

In Kansas all who come there are perfectly free to regulate their own social relations. There has never been a man there who was an abolitionist—for what was there to be abolished? People there had perfect freedom to express what they wished on the subject, when the Nebraska bill was first passed.

Our friends in the South, who support Buchanan, have five disunion men to one at the North. This disunion is a sectional question. Who is to blame for it? Are we? I don't care how you express it.

This government is sought to be put on a new track. Slavery is to be made a ruling element in our government. The question can be avoided in but two ways. By the one, we must submit, and allow slavery to triumph, or, by the other, we must triumph over the black demon. We have chosen the latter manner. If you of the North wish to get rid of this question, you must decide between these two ways—submit and vote for Buchanan, submit and vote that slavery is a just and good thing, and immediately get rid of the question; or unite with us, and help to triumph. We would all like to have the question done away with, but we cannot submit.

They tell us that we are in company with men who have long been known as abolitionists. What care we how many may feel disposed to labor for our cause? Why do not you, Buchanan men, come in and use your influence to make our party respectable?

(Laughter)

How is the dissolution of the Union to be consummated? They tell us that the Union is in danger. Who will divide it? Is it those who make the charge? Are they themselves the persons who wish to see the result? A majority will never dissolve the Union. Can a minority do it?

When this Nebraska bill was first introduced into Congress, the sense of the Democratic party was outraged. That party has ever prided itself, that it *was the friend of individual, universal freedom. It was that principle upon which they carried their measures. When the Kansas scheme was conceived, it was natural that this respect and sense should have been outraged.*

Now I make this appeal to the Democratic citizens here. Don't you find yourself making arguments in support of these measures, which you never would have made before? Did you ever do it before this Nebraska bill compelled you to do it? If you answer this in the affirmative, see how a whole party has been turned away from their love of liberty!

And now, my Democratic friends, come forward. Throw off these things, and come to the rescue of the great principle of equality. Don't interfere with anything in the Constitution. That must be maintained, for it is the only safeguard of our liberties. And not to Democrats alone do I make this appeal, but to all who love these great and true principles. Come, and keep coming! Strike, and strike again! So sure as God lives, the victory shall be yours.

(Great cheering)

Lincoln proved to be a powerful speaker and was well received by the community.

Now, just where was the platform from which Lincoln gave his address in Bronson Park? The exact locations of the four platforms is not specifically known. Were they at each of the four corners, or were they at each of the four sides of the park? There is a Michigan historical marker near the southwest corner of the park, and the text simply states that Lincoln made a speech there. There is also a boulder with a bronze plaque located near Rose Street.

The boulder with the bronze plaque was erected sometime between 1925 and 1935 by the Sarah E. Fuller Tent No. 8 Daughters of Union Veterans of the Civil War. The text states: "This boulder is placed on the spot where Abraham Lincoln stood when he gave an anti-slavery address in August 1856."

As a local chapter of the Daughters of Union Veterans, the group would have known all of the surviving veterans of the Civil War who resided in Kalamazoo County and many of the older residents who recalled Lincoln's visit. Among those there would, undoubtedly, have been someone who remembered Lincoln's speech and where the platform was located. Those members of the Daughters of Union Veterans who placed the monument would most likely have made a concerted effort to correctly position the boulder. Of course, this is all speculation but certainly makes for a good

Daughters of Union Veterans of the Civil War monument, Bronson Park. *Photo by the author.*

argument. Unfortunately, no records from the Daughter's Tent No. 8 have been located.

During the winter of 2019, the placement of the boulder became a moot point, as the City of Kalamazoo moved all veteran-related monuments and memorials residing in Bronson Park to a Memorial Walk located at the east end of the park along Rose Street.

3

THE WAR COMES TO KALAMAZOO COUNTY

Climax is attempting to form its own company & drill x2 per week. We shall keep up our organization until something turns up and perfect ourselves as far as possible in the drill. Went out to Schoolcraft on Saturday to see their company.
—*Letter from Sam Hodgman to his brother Frank, May 21, 1861*

When, in the election of 1860, Abraham Lincoln was chosen president of the United States, the planter class decided that it would not abide by the Constitution and recognize the legitimacy of the election. The news of the fall of Fort Sumter on April 13, 1861, was presumably a shock to the citizens of the county of Kalamazoo. That shock soon turned to action. Over the several proceeding months, actions taken by the Republican Party in the United States Congress worked to appease the Southern slave-holding Democrats.

On April 15, 1861, a meeting of several of Kalamazoo's prominent citizens was held in the law office of J.W. Bruce. Among those in attendance were Samuel Walbridge; Frederick Curtenius, a veteran of the Mexican-American War of 1848; Attorney Dwight May; United States senator Charles Stuart; Israel Kellogg; General Isaac Moffat, a veteran of the War of 1812; and Judge Hezekiah Wells. It was decided that a public meeting should be held the next day in Firemen's Hall.

Fireman's Hall, located on Burdick Street, was a two-story building constructed in 1853. It was eighty-two feet by forty-one feet and thirty-four feet in height, including the bell tower. The bell was used as the village

Fireman's Hall, located on Burdick Street. *From a map at the Kalamazoo Public Library.*

fire alarm. The basement was divided into stalls for use as a city market. On the second or main floor was a room for large gatherings to be used as space for meetings of the several local organizations, including the Ladies Library Association. The *Kalamazoo Gazette* described the interior of the upper floor meeting hall during its construction: "This room will be eighty feet in length by forty feet in width, and twenty-two feet in height. It is to be furnished with moveable seats that can be cleared away in a few moments time, and a clear floor left in the event of its being wanted at any time for a festival or ball."

On the night of April 16, a public meeting, open to all residents of Kalamazoo County, was called to order by Senator Stuart. He gave a stirring speech, reviewing the previous eighty years of the history of the nation and how it grew and the prosperity that it enjoyed. He then turned the attention of the citizens to the threat of upheaval to their duly constituted republic. Senator Stuart hoped that the tenor of the meeting would be a desire for peace, until all avenues for a consolatory end were exhausted. He also stated that if war came, it would be the duty of Michigan and the villages of the county to respond to President Lincoln's call for troops. His remarks were constantly interrupted with thunderous applause from the audience.

The next speaker was David A. Fisher, another veteran of the Mexican-American War. He gave an impassioned account of his dedication to the preservation of the Union and closed his patriotic comments with the statement that if it was necessary to give his life for the country, "he hoped the 'Star-Spangled Banner' would be his burial shroud."

A committee was appointed by Senator Stuart to draft a resolution to express the sentiments of the citizens of Kalamazoo. The committee members were Joseph Miller, Hezekiah G. Wells, Fredrick W. Curtenius, Marsh Giddings, James P. Woodbury, Dwight May, Samuel E. Walbridge, William Mottram, John W. Breese, John Dudgeon, E.H. Davis, Gilbert Wilson and Thomas Cobb. The resolution stated:

> *Resolved, That this is the duty of the Governor of this State to respond to the proclamation of the President of the United States, and to take such action either a respect to legislation or otherwise as shall be necessary to enable the State of Michigan to discharge her whole duty in her present crisis.*
>
> *Resolved, that in common with all good and patriotic citizens, we most sincerely lament the present disturbed condition of our country. That to uphold its Constitution, obey its laws, and sustain its constituted authorities, is but the plain duty of all its citizens, and one which should always be performed promptly and cheerfully. That we, the people of Kalamazoo, here assembled, hereby pledge to each other and to our fellow countrymen the faithful discharge of all such obligations.*

The resolution was unanimously adopted.

Tensions Run High

Leading up to the beginning of the Civil War, the congressional Republicans became weary of being taken advantage of by the Southern Democrats. An example of the lengths the slaveholding faction was willing to take culminated in the physical attack on Senator Charles Sumner of Massachusetts by Senator Preston Brooks of South Carolina. On May 20, 1856, Sumner had given a speech on the floor of the Senate in support of Kansas being admitted to the Union as long as it was a free state. Sumner took the opportunity to condemn the institution of slavery and personally called out Brooks and members of his family, suggesting Brooks's reasons for his continued defense of it was to afford slave owners the opportunity to prey upon female slaves. Brooks was infuriated.

On May 22, after the session had ended and the chamber was almost empty, Brooks approached Sumner as he was sitting at his desk in the Senate and began to beat him on the head with his heavy cane. Sumner tried to defend himself by falling to the floor under his desk, to no avail. Other senators tried to come to Sumner's aid but were blocked by two other Democrats, who were armed with pistols. The beating of Sumner was so severe that he almost died and was not able to return to his seat in the Senate for three years.

In the summer of 1861, the Democrats of Kalamazoo County were still clinging to the notion that outright war could be avoided. They promoted "peace and conciliation" and professed to be against "coercion and war." A meeting was called to be held on Saturday, August 17, 1861, at one o'clock in Vicksburg. The speakers were Dr. Foster Pratt, a local physician, and Nathanial A. Balch, the former prosecuting attorney of Kalamazoo County. The event was reported on in the *Kalamazoo Gazette*, which told of the participation of some unwelcome visitors: "From Kalamazoo, from Centreville, from Mendon, from Schoolcraft, and from Wakeshma and all the surrounding country, the MOB came…one senator, two former senators, a regent of the university, a postmaster, one sheriff, one former sheriff, one county clerk, no lawyers, three doctors, three abolition priests, several deacons, many members of churches, drunkards, thieves, black legs by the score."

Apparently, those loyal to the Union and supportive of President Lincoln felt that rebel sympathizers were not going to be tolerated in Kalamazoo County. The Democrat speakers were constantly shouted down. Dr. Pratt asked those gathered, "Do you propose to permit a rabble from Kalamazoo to come down here to dictate to you, who you shall hear, and who you shall not hear?"

One man in the crowd shouted out, "We ain't all from Kalamazoo!"

At one point, George Winslow, a monument cutter from Kalamazoo, stood on a wheel of the wagon being used as a speaker's platform and asked if the Democrats would be willing to take an oath of allegiance. He proposed that the county clerk, Daniel Cahill, administer the oath, which stated, "That we will support the Constitution and the laws of this state, the Constitution and laws of the United States, and that we will give a cordial and hearty support to the administration of President Lincoln, in the vigorous prosecution of the war to a successful termination, so help me God."

Dr. Pratt, speaking on behalf of the Democrats assembled, declined to take the oath as presented.

During the proceedings, Orrin N. Giddings, former county treasurer who represented Kalamazoo County in the Michigan legislature in 1847, related a conversation he had with Dr. Pratt the previous day, during which Dr. Pratt had "expressed pleasure over the defeats of the Union Army." There were calls from the crowd to hang Dr. Pratt as a traitor.

Outnumbered four to one, the Democrats decided to end the meeting. Drs. Smith and Pratt left the grounds and went to Dr. Smith's home, followed by the Union men. A meeting was held in the house, and a resolution was adopted, which included, "In the fratricidal war with our brethren of other states, presents one of the darkest pages of the world's history, as it might have been, and ought to have been prevented by conciliation and compromise."

By 1862, the Democrats of the county either had a change of heart or decided that a demonstration of their loyalty to the Union was needed. Several Democrats, including Foster Pratt, volunteered to serve in the 13th Michigan Infantry. Dr. Pratt was commissioned as the regimental surgeon.

Senator Brooks was never charged with a crime or held accountable for his attack on Senator Sumner, save for a censure from the Senate floor.

4

Kalamazoo Prepares for War

Almost every young man and some married men have enlisted.
The quota is nearly, if not quite full from this town.
—Moses Hodgman of Climax, August 29, 1862

Charles S. May, the prosecuting attorney of the village, received a commission from Michigan governor Austin Blair to raise a company of men to serve in a Michigan infantry regiment. By 4:00 p.m. on April 22, 1861, there were twenty-five names on that roster. Simultaneously, Sheriff Benjamin Orcutt was drilling fifty men on the second floor of the Humphrey Block.

The April 26, 1861 edition of the *Kalamazoo Gazette* described the patriotic feeling in the village: "Red, White & Blue is the favorite color just now; flags are flying from all public buildings, hotels, stores and many private residences—there is a perfect mass meeting about the recruiting offices. It is said that these companies will be raised in the village readily."

The Kalamazoo Light Guard was the local militia company in Kalamazoo. It would meet on a monthly basis to train, drill and parade through the streets of the town. The light guard maintained an armory, located on the second floor of the Humphrey Block at the southeast corner of Michigan Avenue and Portage Street. This building, erected in 1855, still stands today and is the current home of the Olde Peninsula Brewpub. Muskets, cartridge boxes, ammunition and equipment were stored there. The light guard, originally clad in gray uniforms with black trim, would have to quickly change to

Kalamazoo Prepares for War

Humphrey Block, corner of Michigan Avenue and Portage Street. *Photo by the author.*

Union blue. When the unit was accepted into the state service, it would be designated Company I and mustered into the 2nd Michigan Infantry on May 25, 1861. The second company to organize was the Kalamazoo Blair Guard, named for Governor Blair. This company, when mustered into the service of the state, would be designated Company K of the 2nd Michigan.

The first Kalamazoo resident to enlist for the war was a young man, only seventeen years old, by the name of William Shakespeare. William enlisted on April 12, 1861, as a corporal in Company K, 2nd Michigan Infantry. He would see service with the 2nd until he was wounded in action on July 11, 1863.

The National Driving Park, located in the current boundaries of the Washington Square neighborhood, was a nationally famous track for harness racing. Owners and drivers came from all across the United States to prove who had the fastest horse. Built in 1858, the Driving Park also served as the county fairgrounds, and when the circus came to town, the environs would almost burst with humanity. The horse stables, at first being used as barracks for the new recruits, were soon at capacity. A tent city was then erected. The infield of the track became the training ground, and the soldiers learned to march and were drilled for hours in the warm spring sun. With this many men and boys coming together and doing their best to become some semblance of soldiers, accidents and illness were inevitable. The armory space in the Humphrey Block building was converted into a makeshift infirmary, as there would not be a regular hospital in Kalamazoo for another twenty-eight years.

Between August 1861 and June 1862, no less than five recruiting offices sprang up in the village. The 16th United States Infantry opened an office in the brick block opposite the post office. The 1st Michigan Cavalry was in the Burdick House Hotel on Main Street. The 13th Michigan Infantry was in offices over L.W. Perrin's store, located on the corner of Main (Michigan Avenue) and Burdick Street. The 17th Michigan Infantry was on the corner of Main and Burdick Streets, and the 18th United States Infantry had an office somewhere in the city; the location was not recorded.

The board of supervisors of Kalamazoo County met on May 6, 1861, and voted by resolution to set aside $3,000 as its contribution to the support of those willing to enlist, "for paying for board and other expenses of companies I and K of the 2nd Regiment Michigan Volunteers, while said companies were being enrolled, and also in providing for the support of children, or females, that may be dependant [sic] for support on any of the volunteers, residents of this county, who have or may go into the service of the State under the order of the Governor and Adjutant General of Michigan."

The Casualties Begin

It was not very long after the excitement and flurry of preparations for war began that the reality of the situation grasped the village. Death in its grim form visited the ranks of the eager enlistees encamped at the racetrack.

As the Light Guard was drilling on the fairgrounds that spring, Henry Carrier, a twenty-one-year-old tinsmith, caught a cold, which most likely turned into pneumonia. In a letter to the *Kalamazoo Daily Telegraph* dated May 31, 1876, Mr. Oliver H. Perry, himself a veteran of the 5th Michigan Cavalry, wrote:

> *The First Who Fell.*
> *Henry Carrier, a young man employed by Walker, Sanger and Edwards as a tinner, enlisted in Capt. D. (Dwight) May's Company I, 2nd Regiment.*

Headstone of Henry Carrier, Mountain Home Cemetery. *Photo by the author.*

While the company were drilling upon the old fair ground, Henry caught a severe cold which resulted in congestion, and finally in his death, which occurred at Mrs. Perry's, then living on Academy street. Mr. Carrier's grave is unknown as a soldier, but he is as much entitled to the honors as any that fell. Let us place his record upon a good substantial tablet, that in the years to come he may be remembered.

There is no official record of Henry's death in the ledgers of the village or the county. As he was never officially mustered into the service of the state of Michigan, he is not listed in the official records of the regiment. Henry lies buried at Mountain Home Cemetery. Someone heeded Mr. Perry's suggestion because sometime later a marble headstone, a good substantial tablet, appeared on his grave. This privately purchased marble headstone tells of his sacrifice:

Henry B. Carrier
AE. 21.
First to fall of Kalamazoo Volunteers.
Enlisted for Co. I, 2nd Michigan Infantry.

All Roads Lead from Kalamazoo County

Kalamazoo's two companies were accepted by the state and admitted to the 2nd Michigan Infantry. Company I was commanded by Captain Dwight May. The other commissioned officers were First Lieutenant William J. Handy, also of Kalamazoo, and Second Lieutenant John M. Norvell of Detroit. Captain Charles S. May, brother of Dwight, commanded Company K, with First Lieutenant George W. Park and Second Lieutenant Harry C. Church, both of Kalamazoo.

After leaving Kalamazoo, the two companies of the 2nd Michigan went into camp as a regiment at the state fairgrounds in Detroit and then moved to Fort Wayne, which still stands today. The 2nd Michigan's first commanding officer was Colonel Israel B. Richardson of Pontiac. He would eventually be promoted to major general and command a division in the Army of the Potomac, only to be mortally wounded in Miller's Cornfield at the Battle of Antietam in Sharpsburg, Maryland, on September 17, 1862.

The 2nd Michigan left Fort Wayne and went to Washington, D.C. The 2nd "first saw the elephant," a soldier's term for seeing his first battle, on July 18, 1861, at Blackburn's Ford, Virginia. Over the next four years, these Kalamazoo County boys would see action in some of the bloodiest fighting of the war, including First Bull Run (Manassas), White Oak Swamp, Malvern Hill and Fredericksburg, all in Virginia. In 1863, the 2nd was transferred to the western theater of the war and fought in Vicksburg and Jackson, Mississippi, as well as Lenoir Station and Knoxville, Tennessee. In 1864, the regiment was back in Virginia at places like the Wilderness, Spotsylvania, North Anna, the Siege of Petersburg, Weldon Railroad and Hatcher's Run. The 2nd Michigan Infantry was present at the surrender of Robert E. Lee and the Army of Northern Virginia on April 9, 1865.

A total of 1,818 men and one woman served in the 2nd Michigan. That one woman was Sarah Edmunds, known to her comrades as Franklin Thompson, who enlisted in Flint, Michigan. Sarah was able to pass herself off as a young man for almost two years, until contracting malaria. Fearing she would be discovered if she went to the hospital, she made her way to Ohio and assumed her own identity. After the war, many of the soldiers pressured their legislators in Washington, and Congress passed an act to allow Sarah a pension of twelve dollars per month for her "splendid record as a soldier, unblemished character, and disabilities incurred."

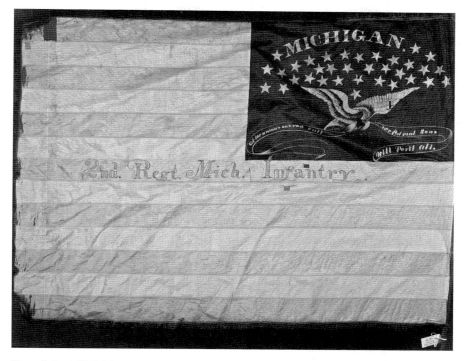

Flag of the 2nd Michigan Infantry. *Photo by Peter Glendinning; courtesy of Save the Flags, Michigan Capital Committee.*

The 2nd participated in the Grand Review of the Union armies at Washington, D.C., on May 23, 1865. The regiment was mustered out of service on July 28 and finally arrived at Detroit on August 1.

Besides the two companies of the 2nd Michigan Infantry that were raised in Kalamazoo in 1861, four regiments of infantry, one regiment of cavalry, one regiment of sharpshooters and one artillery battery were encamped and trained at different times in Kalamazoo at the National Race Track.

6TH MICHIGAN INFANTRY

The 6th Michigan Infantry was commanded by Colonel Frederick W. Curtenius, a prominent citizen of Kalamazoo, who served as a captain in the Mexican-American War. The regiment was mustered into service on

Flag of the 6th Michigan Infantry. *Photo by Peter Glendinning; courtesy of Save the Flags, Michigan Capital Committee.*

August 20, 1861. By the summer of 1863, it was also referred to as the 6th Michigan Heavy Artillery. Heavy artillery cannons were stationary and fixed in place, commonly in permanent forts on land and along seacoasts. The ten-inch Columbiad in Kalamazoo's Bronson Park is typical of a heavy artillery gun.

Kalamazoo Prepares for War

Colonel Frederick W. Curtenius commanded the 6th Michigan Infantry. *Kalamazoo Valley Museum Collection.*

In the Record of Service of the 6th Michigan Infantry, published by the State of Michigan in 1905, there appears this explanation of the change from Infantry to Artillery:

> *While the Sixth expected to become a part of the Army of the Potomac, the fortunes of war placed most of its service in the southwest, on the Mississippi River and Gulf of Mexico. The regiment was recruited for the infantry arm of the service and served as such until July, 1863, when General Banks converted it into a regiment of heavy artillery on account of its valuable and faithful service, his official order stating that the regiment is "to retain, until otherwise officially designated, its infantry number, and to have the organization, pay, clothing, and equipment prescribed by law and regulations for troops of the artillery arm." The regiment therefore is frequently referred to as the "Sixth Infantry" and also as the "Sixth Heavy Artillery."*

The 6th took part in actions including Vicksburg, Mississippi, Baton Rouge, Louisiana, Port Hudson and the Siege of Mobile, Alabama. Of the total 1,992 who served in the regiment, 4 were killed in action, 2 died of wounds, 13 died in Confederate prisons and 432 died of disease.

13TH MICHIGAN INFANTRY

The 13th Michigan Infantry was raised by United States senator Charles E. Stuart and commanded by Colonel Michael Shoemaker of Jackson. It was nicknamed the "Michigan Rifles" and was known as "Kalamazoo's Own."

While the 13th was in camp at the National Race Track, several residents of Kalamazoo desired to provide the regiment with a suitable set of flags, a regimental and a United States, or federal, flag. Unfortunately, the flags were on special order from a firm in New York City and did not arrive in Kalamazoo before the regiment left for Kentucky. An account from *Michigan in the War* describes the situation:

> *When they were received, they were at once sent forward and presented "sans ceremonie," at Nashville, Tennessee, on dress parade, February 12, 1862. They were of elegant silk and fine workmanship, with the inscription in gold letters, "Presented by the citizens of Kalamazoo to the 13th Michigan Infantry." When the regiment returned to Kalamazoo on veteran furlough in February, 1864, the flags were formally returned to the donors in an appropriate and earnest address by Surgeon Foster Pratt, and were received on behalf of the village authorities by the Hon. H.G. Wells. They have since been delivered in the care of the State for deposit with the other war flags in the State Capital.*

The 13th's regimental flag was unique. Instead of being made of dark blue silk, like most Michigan Infantry regimental colors, the silk was light blue. The obverse featured the coat of arms of the state of Michigan. Above this are the words "Presented by the Citizens of Kalamazoo to the," and below the coat of arms in a red scroll, "13th Michigan Infantry."

The 13th left Kalamazoo on February 12, 1862, and arrived at the battlefield of Shiloh, Tennessee, the day after the battle. Some of the battles it participated in were the Siege of Corinth, Mississippi; Perryville, Kentucky; Stone's River, Tennessee; Lookout Mountain, Tennessee; Chickamauga, Georgia; Chattanooga, Tennessee; Mission Ridge, Tennessee; Savannah, Georgia; and Bentonville, North Carolina. It also participated in Sherman's famous March to the Sea and the Grand Review at Washington, D.C., in May 1865. It had on its rolls 2,092 men. Of these, 47 were killed in action, 33 died of wounds, 7 died in Confederate prisons and 253 died of disease. The 13th Michigan Infantry was mustered out of service on July 25, 1865.

Kalamazoo Prepares for War

Captain Clement C. Webb of Kalamazoo was in command of Company E, 13th Michigan Infantry. He died on February 16, 1863, of wounds received at the battle of Stones River, Tennessee, on December 31, 1862. *Kalamazoo Valley Museum Collection.*

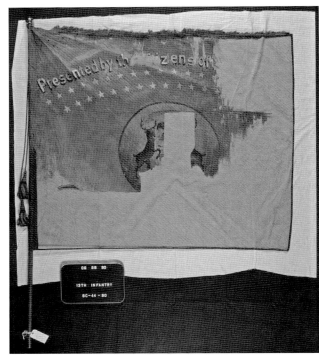

Left: Regimental flag of the 13th Michigan Infantry. *Photo by Peter Glendinning; courtesy of Save the Flags, Michigan Capital Committee.*

Below: Reproduction of the 13th Michigan Infantry regimental flag. *Courtesy of Michael Culp; photo by the author.*

Opposite: Reproduction of the 13th Michigan Infantry federal flag. *Courtesy of Michael Culp; photo by the author.*

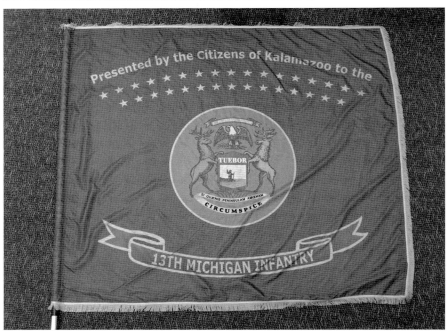

25TH MICHIGAN INFANTRY

The 25th Michigan Infantry was organized on September 22, 1862, at Kalamazoo. It was commanded by Colonel Orlando H. Moore, a native of Schoolcraft, who had served as the lieutenant colonel of the 13th Michigan Infantry. The 25th's most famous engagement took place at the Green River Bridge at Tebb's Bend, near Campellsville, Kentucky. The Record of Service of the 25th Michigan Infantry related this incident:

> *Colonel Moore, with five companies of his regiment, numbering about 200 men, was ordered June 10th to Green River Bridge, near Columbia, as news had been received that the confederate General John Morgan was about to cross the Cumberland River and march on Louisville. Colonel Moore selected his own ground to meet the enemy, supposed to be 3,000 strong, and disposed his small force to combat ten times his number at Tebb's Bend, and fearlessly awaited the approach of the confederates, knowing that no other Union troops were within 30 miles of his camp. The Colonel selected a strong position with the practical eye of a soldier, the flanks of his camp being protected by the river so the enemy was*

Left: Recruiting poster for the 25th Michigan Infantry. *Kalamazoo Valley Museum Collection*.

Right: Colonel Orlando Moore, commanding officer of the 25th Michigan Infantry at Tebb's Bend, Kentucky. *Kalamazoo Valley Museum Collection*.

compelled to meet him in front, and strengthened it by throwing up a line of earth works and felling trees to protect his men against the charge of the enemy's cavalry. On the morning of July 4, 1863, the forces of General Morgan opened with musketry and artillery upon the little band of Union troops and after Colonel Moore's skirmishers had been driven in a flag of truce approached with a demand from General Morgan for an immediate and unconditional surrender.

Colonel Moore met the flag of truce and sent back a message, stating, "Present my compliments to General Morgan and say to him that, this being the Fourth of July, I cannot entertain the proposition of surrender."

The Confederates immediately charged the camp, and a desperate conflict raged for four hours, with the overwhelming numbers of the enemy surging up so close to the Union lines that they were driven back repeatedly in a hand-to-hand encounter. General Morgan, seeing the hopelessness of continuing the conflict longer, withdrew his forces after he had met with a loss of as many killed and wounded as Colonel Moore had in his command. Twenty-two of the Confederate commissioned officers were killed or

Flag of the 25th Michigan Infantry. *Photo by Peter Glendinning; courtesy of Save the Flags, Michigan Capital Committee.*

wounded. Among the killed was Colonel Chenault and Major Brent, while Colonel Moore lost six killed and twenty-three wounded.

The Confederate forces attacked the 25th Michigan a total of eight times and were repulsed each time. Two hundred rebel soldiers were killed during the encounter. Major General Hartsuff, in a general order, complimented Colonel Moore and the officers and men of his command, saying, "The entire arrangement of his defense entitles him to the highest credit for military skill. The obstinate defense made by Colonel Moore and his men delayed General Morgan twelve hours, which completely frustrated his plan of march and undoubtedly saved the city of Louisville from being looted by Morgan's men and the destruction of vast stores for the Union army."

There were actually 260 men of the 25th Michigan entrenched at Tebb's Bend. Undoubtedly, many of those men were from Kalamazoo.

The 25th's total enrollment was 1,008 soldiers, of which 23 were killed in action, 17 died of wounds, 2 died in prisoner of war camps and 126 died of disease. Today, on the island in the middle of Lane Boulevard in the Washington Square neighborhood, there sits a large rock with a plaque commemorating the 25th Michigan Infantry.

28th Michigan Infantry

The 28th Michigan Infantry was created by consolidating the companies for the 28th Michigan Infantry, which, at the time, was forming at Marshall, Michigan, and the 29th Michigan Infantry, which was organizing in Kalamazoo. The companies of both units totaled 886 officers and enlisted men when the consolidation was completed on October 26, 1864. That same day, the regiment left Kalamazoo by railroad and proceeded south to Kentucky and then on to Tennessee. The 28th took part in the Battle of Nashville, Tennessee, from December 12 to 16 and defended its position on the battlefield against attacks by General John Bell Hood's Texans.

In January 1865, the regiment was ordered back north to Louisville, Kentucky. Shortly thereafter, the 28th went to Alexandria, Virginia. From there, the soldiers boarded navel transports and headed south to North Carolina. Near Kingston, North Carolina, the regiment took part in the battle of Wyse Forks and were in the heaviest of the fighting. The 28th lost 7 killed and 13 wounded. It served as occupation forces in the area until it was ordered to Detroit and mustered out on June 8, 1866. During its short term of service, the regiment, in addition to the deaths in action, lost 101 men to disease.

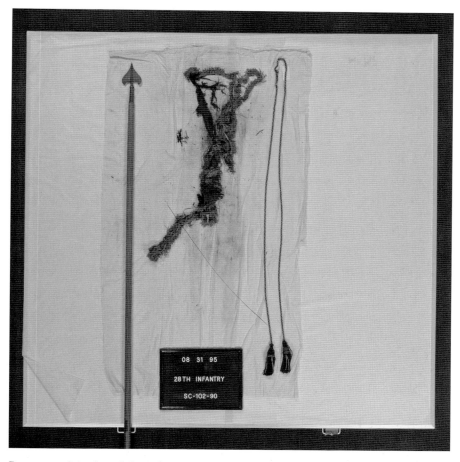

Remnants of the flag of the 28th Michigan Infantry. *Photo by Peter Glendinning; courtesy of Save the Flags, Michigan Capital Committee.*

11TH MICHIGAN CAVALRY

The 11th Michigan Cavalry was organized at Kalamazoo and was mustered on December 10, 1863. Simeon B. Brown of St. Clair, Michigan, was appointed colonel by Governor Austin Blair.

The 11th left Kalamazoo on December 17, 1863, with 920 officers and men, and headed for Kentucky, where it was assigned to the Army of the Ohio. Its primary assignment was to seek out and destroy the Confederate cavalry that was pursuing guerilla warfare–type attacks against Union forces.

The most troublesome of these was John Hunt Morgan, who led one of the most famous of these units. The 11th and Morgan fought at Mount Sterling and Cynthia, Kentucky, where the 11th was able to push Morgan and his men from the area and into the mountains. In a letter, cavalryman James Nickerson of Schoolcraft described the tenacity shown by the 11th in its pursuit of Morgan, stating, "We make the sons of b—s hunt their holes like rats."

The History of the 11th Michigan Cavalry, published by the State of Michigan, has this account of perhaps the most important service that the regiment performed:

> *In September the regiment participated in the raid into Western Virginia under General Burbridge for the purpose of destroying the extensive salt works located at Saltville, Va. These works were the largest in the confederacy and the confederate government took ample means to guard and protect them, for their destruction would mean a severe loss to the southern armies. General Burbridge's forces consisted of less than 5,000 mounted men and six pieces of artillery, while General Breckenridge in command at Saltville, had upwards of 25,000 men well placed behind strong fortifications. General Burbridge's march was rapid through a broken and mountainous country and he reached the salt works October 2, after skirmishing with the enemy almost continually while in the mountains. The three brigades of the union troops were sent forward in a charge upon the enemy's works, the points of attack being at different places, but they were so vastly outnumbered by the Confederates who stood behind their entrenchments that the charge was hopeless. It was made with spirit and dash, but was soon repulsed, the Eleventh losing in killed, wounded and missing 86 men. Lieutenant Colonel Mason, who led the regiment, was killed.*

At Pulaski, Tennessee, on July 20, 1865, the 11th Michigan Cavalry was consolidated with the 8th Michigan Cavalry and continued its service throughout North Carolina until the war was over. The officers and men were mustered out at Nashville, Tennessee, on September 22, 1865, and returned to Jackson, Michigan, on September 28, 1865. During its less than two years of service, the regiment fought the Confederate forces in fifty-eight different battles and skirmishes from Lexington, Kentucky, to Roanoke, Virginia, and from Salisbury, North Carolina, to Bristol, Tennessee. The total number of men mustered into the regiment was 1,375. Of those, 18 were killed in action, 5 died of their wounds, 2 died in Confederate prisons and 22 died of disease.

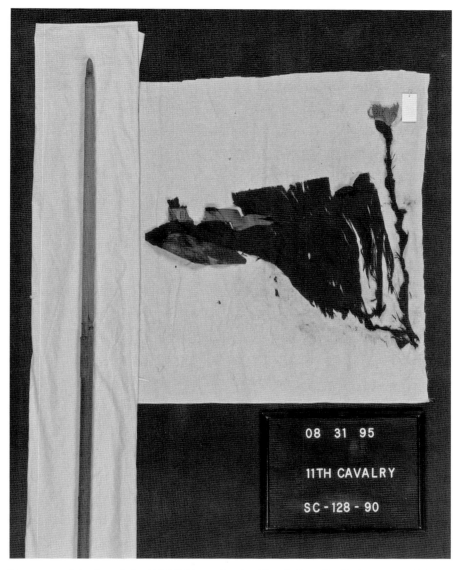

Remnants of the flag of the 11th Michigan Cavalry. *Photo by Peter Glendinning; courtesy of Save the Flags, Michigan Capital Committee.*

14th Battery

Something like a third wheel, the 14th Battery was independent of the 1st Michigan Light Artillery regiment. Standard artillery regiments were structured to have only twelve batteries, so the two additional batteries that were organized in Michigan were designated by numbers. Each battery had six cannons and 100 men. The 14th was organized and mustered into the United States service on January 5, 1864. On February 1, it left Kalamazoo and was sent to Camp Barry at Washington, D.C., an artillery training camp. The battery was supplied with horses, caissons and cannon on April 20 and on May 15 was sent to Fort Bunker Hill, one of a string of fortifications surrounding Washington. Only a week later, on May 22, the battery was sent back to Camp Barry and relieved of its horses. The plan was that the battery would remain in Washington and not be sent into the field. In July, the 14th was in action near Fort Stevens, when Washington was attacked by Confederate general Jubal Early's troops over a three-day period. The rebel assaults were repulsed, and they moved on. By the fall of 1864, the battery was divided into three sections of two guns each. One section was sent to Fort Bunker Hill, one to Fort Totton and the third to Fort Slemmer, all part of the defenses of Washington. It was then that the artillerymen were reassigned, much like the men of the 6th Michigan Infantry, to become heavy artillery. The three sections of the 14th Battery remained in Washington, moving around to several of the other forts, until June 17, 1865, when it was sent to Jackson, Michigan, and mustered out of service. Of the 225 officers and men of the battery, 9 died of disease. None were lost in action.

1st Michigan Sharpshooters

In the fall of 1862, the 1st Michigan Sharpshooters began to organize at the National Race Track at the same time as the 13th Michigan Infantry was organizing. Charles V. DeLand of Jackson was commissioned colonel. It is interesting to note that none of the commissioned officers were from Kalamazoo. The following spring, the regiment was moved to Dearborn. On July 7, 1863, only six companies were mustered into service. The remaining four would be gradually integrated to complete the rolls. Company K, recruited in northern Michigan at Grand Traverse and Lelanau, were all Native Americans.

Flag of the 1st Michigan Light Artillery. *Photo by Peter Glendinning; courtesy of Save the Flags, Michigan Capital Committee.*

News of cavalry commander general John Hunt Morgan leading his horsemen into Ohio and Indiana reached Dearborn quickly. Colonel DeLand was ordered to take his six companies by railroad to Indianapolis and from there southeast to the town of Seymour to try to intercept Morgan's men. The rebels had been looting and burning towns across Ohio

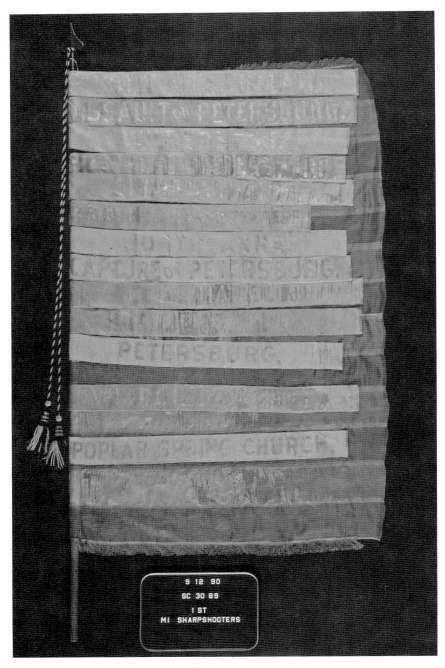

Remnants of the flag of the 1st Michigan Sharpshooters. *Photo by Peter Glendinning; courtesy of Save the Flags, Michigan Capital Committee.*

and Indiana; their latest target was the town of Dupre Station, Indiana, which was devastated.

Morgan and his men eventually made their way to the town of North Vernon, about twenty miles east of Seymour. On July 12, Morgan was in the process of negotiating with the town, making certain demands in order to spare North Vernon from meeting the same fate as many other communities. Colonel DeLand, ignoring the flag of truce, marched his men right into the town, forcing the Confederate delegation to flee. DeLand had only 400 men, and Morgan had 2,200. Knowing this, DeLand contrived a scheme to lull the Confederates into believing that reinforcements had arrived. The rebels made their escape under cover of darkness, leaving only a small force as a rear guard. The sharpshooters forced their way into the camp and captured the remaining rebels. After learning that the whole thing had been a ruse, one Confederate officer exclaimed, "We could have whipped you in ten minutes!" Morgan and his men made their way into Ohio, and the 1st Michigan Sharpshooters saved the town of North Vernon.

The sharpshooters would also see action—all in Virginia—at places like the Wilderness, Spottsylvania, Petersburg, Weldon Railroad and Fort Steadman. At the end of the war, the regiment would be sent first to Washington, D.C., to participate in the Grand Review and then on to Jackson, Michigan. There, it was mustered out of service on August 7, 1865.

The total complement of the 1st Michigan Sharpshooters was 1,206 officers and men. Of those, 69 were killed in battle, 42 died of wounds, 62 of disease and 41 died as prisoners of war, including thirty-seven-year-old Benjamin Freeman of Kalamazoo, who died at Andersonville. He is buried at grave number 11,500, at Andersonville National Cemetery.

A majority of the federal and regimental flags of Michigan Civil War infantry were a standard six feet, six inches tall and six feet wide and trimmed in gold fringe. The staff or pole they were carried on were nine feet, ten inches, including a finial, usually a spear-point but sometimes an eagle or even a spade. From the top of the pole were, most often, two cords and tassels of complementary colors to the flag. Battle honors, or the names of battles the regiment took part in, were often painted on the regimental flag or, on occasion, painted in the stripes of the federal flag belonging to the unit. The regimental designation could also appear on the center white stripe of the flag.

Cavalry units carried a smaller regimental color that was about two and a half feet tall by two and a half feet wide, again trimmed in gold fringe. The federal flag was a quite often a swallow tail flag. It was common

Grave site of the Unknown Civil War Soldiers, Section E, Riverside Cemetery. *Photo by the author.*

among individual artillery batteries to also carry a swallow tail federal flag—the same size as cavalry—with the battery designation painted on the white stripes.

The first Kalamazoo resident to die in battle was Private Theodore Lemon of Company K, 2nd Michigan Infantry. Theodore was among those who enlisted on May 10, 1861. He was killed in action on May 5, 1862, at the Battle of Williamsburg, Virginia, during the Peninsula Campaign. He was twenty years old. No record of where his is buried has been located.

The first to die of disease was Frank Taylor, also of the 2nd Michigan, a private of Company I. He died on October 11, 1861, at Georgetown, in Washington, D.C. He was twenty-three years old. Frank was married to Miss Charlotte Ann Baxter on February 24, 1861.

Between 1862 and 1864, ten or twelve men, depending on which civil record or newspaper article you look at, died either in camp at the National Race Track or in the armory hospital. The remains of these individuals were taken to the newly established Riverside Cemetery on the east side of the Kalamazoo River. A lot in Section E had been set aside and is referred to in sources as the "U.S. Lot." The identities of these soldiers were lost by 1869 and are listed as unknowns in the official records of the United States government, called the Roll of Honor. It can be assumed that these men were not from the immediate area, because if they were, the families would most likely have marked the graves or at least had the names recorded in the register of burials for the cemetery. To this day, these graves remain unmarked.

5

The Black Community

It is rather lonesome here now that Sam left us last Thursday for the war.
—*Letter from Moses Hodgman to his son Frank, July 2, 1861*

The 1850 census of Kalamazoo County reveals that there were 97 residents of African descent living in the county. Within ten years' time, that number had grown to 305. Of these, 208 resided in the Kalamazoo Village limits. The 1860 census also shows that 23 of these individuals were day laborers. They were not regularly employed, but every morning, they would go from one business or work site to another, inquiring if there was any manual labor for them to perform. They would generally be paid at the end of the day.

Fourteen residents were skilled tradesmen. This included eight barbers, a brick and/or stonemason, two shoemakers, three seamstresses and/or dressmakers and one carpenter. Other occupations listed were six farmers and eight farm laborers, ten washerwomen, a well digger, a hotel waiter and one Baptist preacher, the Reverend Mr. Dooling.

At the outbreak of the Civil War, there were no provisions for men of color to enlist and serve in the army. Many Black men, however, were serving in the United States Navy. Henry Barnes, the editor of the *Detroit Advertiser and Tribune*, continually called for allowing Black men to enlist. He reported that army recruiters from New England had been in Michigan, mostly in Detroit and Battle Creek, signing up young men to serve in a new regiment, the 54th Massachusetts Infantry. The 54th was the subject of the 1989 film *Glory*, starring Morgan Freeman, Matthew Broderick and Denzel Washington. It was not uncommon for recruiters to visit other states when they were having difficulties filling their quotas to complete a regiment. At the same time, the 55th Massachusetts Infantry was being organized, also a Black regiment, as a sister unit to the 54th.

In the summer of 1863, with his frustration at the boiling point, newspaperman Barnes contacted the War Department in Washington, D.C., requesting permission to raise a Black regiment in Michigan. On July 24, 1863, Secretary of War Edwin M. Stanton wrote to Michigan governor Austin Blair, authorizing the organization of such a regiment:

> *GOVERNOR—H. Barns, Esq., of Detroit, has applied to this department for authority to raise a regiment of colored troops in your State. The department is very anxious that such a regiment should be raised, and authorizes you to raise them by volunteering under the regulations of the department, a copy of which is submitted to you by the chief of the bureau, and it would be gratifying if you should give such authority to Mr. Barnes. It seems to me that there has been some misunderstanding upon this subject, and I am informed that you were under the impression that the department would not authorize it. Until suitable arrangements could be made for the organization of a bureau, it was not deemed advisable to raise such troops, but the organization of colored troops is now a distinct bureau in the department, and as fully recognized as any other branch of the military service, and every encouragement is given by the department to the raising of such troops.*
>
> *Yours truly,*
> *Edwin M. Stanton, Secretary of War*

The 1st Michigan Colored Infantry was raised from all across the state. Recruiters set up offices in several cities and towns, including Kalamazoo, to enroll volunteers. Many Black men came from southern Michigan to enlist. Upward of fifty-one men made the trip to Kalamazoo. Several came from Battle Creek, and many from as far away as Cass County were determined to fight for the Union.

The fifty-six volunteers were sent to Camp Ward in Detroit, where they were organized with the other recruits into their companies.

While in Detroit, the volunteers completed their training. In December, a detachment of the regiment, about 250 men, was sent on a trip by railroad across southern Michigan to show the people of the state how well the 1st Michigan Colored Infantry was trained and its readiness for

Flag of the 1st Michigan Colored Infantry/102nd United States Colored Troops. *Photo by Peter Glendinning; courtesy of Save the Flags, Michigan Capital Committee.*

service. During the two week trip, the soldiers made stops in Ypsilanti, Ann Arbor and Jackson, where Governor Austin Blair was quoted in the *Detroit Advertiser and Tribune* when he addressed the men: "This is the first time I ever saw Negro troops, and I am very proud of your general bearing. Take courage, do your duty nobly."

At every stop along the way, the citizens of the several communities welcomed the soldiers with speeches and provided them with meals prepared by the ladies of those communities. The tour continued on to Marshall and then to Kalamazoo, where Lieutenant Governor Dwight May, former captain of the 2nd Michigan Infantry and a resident of the village, reviewed the troops. From Kalamazoo, the train went west to Niles. After spending the night, the troops marched the sixteen miles to Cassopolis, where again, the citizens welcomed the soldiers.

The regiment mustered into service on February 17, 1864. There were 895 officers and men. In March 1864, the 1st Michigan Colored Infantry was assigned to Major General Ambrose E. Burnside's 9th Army Corps. A few weeks later, the regiment left Detroit and traveled by train to Annapolis, Maryland. On April 14, the 1st Michigan Colored Infantry was reviewed by Generals Burnside and Ulysses S. Grant. Both commanders were pleased with the new recruits. General Grant was quoted as saying that they were "splendid."

One of the officers of the 1st Michigan Colored Infantry came from Kalamazoo. Captain Calvin Montague of Company K, whose family built a large brick house on Asylum Avenue (now Oakland Drive), served in the regiment. This house still stands and is part of the Western Michigan University Campus.

The 1st Michigan Colored Infantry left Annapolis for Hilton Head, South Carolina, on April 15. After its arrival, the regiment was transferred from its state regiment designation as the 1st Michigan Colored Infantry and mustered into the federal service as the 102nd United States Colored Troops (USCT).

The 102nd saw action in the battles of Baldwin, Florida, on August 8, 1864; Honey Hill, South Carolina, on November 30, 1864; Tillifinny, South Carolina, on December 7, 1864; Deveaux Neck, South Carolina, on December 9, 1864; Cuckwold's Creek Bridge on February 8, 1865; Sumterville, South Carolina, on April 8, 1865; Spring Hill, South Carolina, on April 15, 1865; Swift Creek, South Carolina, on April 17, 1865; Boykin, South Carolina, on April 18, 1865; and Singleton's plantation on April 19, 1865. In December 1864, the regiment fought a small skirmish with Confederate forces at Grahmsville, South Carolina, and received the highest commendation for holding ground under severe fire and against a charge of the Confederate troops. The regiment continued its service as occupation troops until the fall of 1865.

The 102nd United States Colored Troops was discharged from the service of the United States on September 30, 1865, and made its way back to Detroit, where it was disbanded on October 17, 1865. During its term of service, the regiment lost 5 killed in action, 7 died of wounds, 116 died of disease and 114 were discharged due to disability. The total number of soldiers who served in the regiment during the war was 1,673.

Seven Black men from the Kalamazoo County served in the 102nd, and their stories are as follows.

Lovett Hammond worked as a day laborer to support his growing family. Born in North Carolina in 1830, most likely a slave, he and his wife Rebecca made their way north and, by 1850, were living in Marion County, Indiana. The 1860 census places the Hammond family in Kalamazoo. On March 6, 1865, Lovett enlisted in Company K, 102nd United States Colored Troops for a period of one year. He was thirty-five years old and by then had five children. The 102nd was stationed at Georgetown, South Carolina, when Lovett was sent to join his comrades. He served just over six months, when he was discharged with the regiment on September 30, 1865. Lovett returned home, and his family continued to grow. In all, he and Rebecca had eleven children. Sadly, five of the children would die as teenagers. Lovett died on April 28, 1882, at the age of fifty-two, of consumption. He was a member of the local veteran's organization Orcutt Post No. 79 Grand Amy of the Republic (GAR) and was buried on its lot in Riverside Cemetery. His wife, Rebecca, lived until 1895.

Thomas Woodford, born in 1835 in Kentucky, worked as a day laborer. He enlisted on January 29, 1864, and was twenty-eight years old. Thomas was married and had two daughters and a son at home. He enlisted as a corporal of Company K. He served through the remainder of the war and was discharged at Charleston, South Carolina, on September 30, 1865. Thomas returned to Kalamazoo, and by 1880, he had fathered four more children. One of his sons, George, would die in 1885, at the age of fifteen. His daughter Mary died in 1889, at the age of twenty-two. His daughter Mattie married Benjamin Hammond, the son of Rix Hammond. Thomas died in 1895 and is buried at the Orcutt Post No. 79 GAR lot in Riverside Cemetery.

Rix Hammond was born into slavery in Halifax County, North Carolina, in 1832. On October 27, 1863, his was one of several names drawn from the wooden draft box. He was thirty-one years old. Rix was originally assigned to Company F, 2nd Michigan Cavalry. As far as is known, he is the only Black man to serve in the 2nd Cavalry. He transferred to Company I, 102nd USCT and joined his new regiment on May 31, 1865, at Orangeburg, South Carolina. He was discharged with the rest of the regiment on September 30, 1865, at Charleston, South Carolina. He was mustered out at Detroit, when the 102nd arrived back in Michigan. After the war, Rix returned to

Kalamazoo and his family and took up his job as a laborer. For several years, Rix suffered from the effects of alcoholism, perhaps a result of post-traumatic stress. He applied for and received a soldiers' pension in the amount of twelve dollars per month. The *Kalamazoo Telegraph* reported on May 12, 1894, that "Rix Hammond, a colored man of this city, was found in a lumber yard on Portage Street yesterday, suffering from hemorrhages. He was taken to the Hygeia Sanitarium where he died in twenty minutes. The deceased was 62 years of age."

The death certificate on file in Lansing states that the hemorrhage was in his lungs. The exact cause is unknown, but it is possible that he had contracted tuberculosis. Rix was buried at Riverside Cemetery at section T, lot 46, grave 05, by several of his fellow veterans. There was no other information about the circumstances of his death. It is not known for certain if Rix and Lovett Hammond were related. It seems quite coincidental that they were both born in North Carolina two years apart with the same last name.

Aaron Burnett is listed in the 1860 census of Kalamazoo as an eighteen-year-old laborer, living in the household of John Hardimon. He also stated to the census taker that he was born in Indiana. He enlisted in Company A on September 28, 1863, for three years. He mustered out with the regiment at Charleston, South Carolina, on September 30, 1865. No other information has been found on him.

At the age of forty-five years, Elijah Harris must have felt compelled to enlist to fight for the Union. Born in Tennessee in 1818, he was much older than most of his comrades. He enlisted in Company B on December 30, 1863, at Kalamazoo. He joined the regiment at Beaufort, South Carolina, on October 14, 1863. By May 16, 1865, he was listed on the roster of the sick. It is presumed that he was mustered out with the rest of his regiment on September 30, 1865. Elijah returned to Kalamazoo after the war. Subsequent records show his last name as Harrison. Even his government-supplied marble headstone is inscribed Elijah Harrison. Elijah died in January 1875, at the age of fifty-seven. He was buried at Section A of Riverside Cemetery.

It is apparent that Edward Kersey was a determined young man. Born in Indiana, he, his mother and siblings took up residence in Pavilion Township, Kalamazoo County, before 1860. Edward made his way to Detroit after hearing the news that there would be a Black regiment from the state. Only eighteen when he enlisted on October 8, 1863, Edward most likely could read and write, because when he was mustered into the 1st Michigan Colored Infantry, he was appointed sergeant. On February 20, 1864, Edward was promoted to first sergeant, a position of great responsibility in Company

Left: Grave of Albert Whaling, the last Black veteran of Kalamazoo, on the GAR lot, Riverside Cemetery. *Photo by the author.*

Below: United States Colored Troops Monument, Nashville National Cemetery, Nashville, Tennessee. *Photo by the author.*

The Black Community

C. On December 9, 1864, at the battle of Deveaux Neck, South Carolina, Edward was wounded. How and where he was wounded is not known; however, it might not have been too bad, as he was not discharged until the regiment was disbanded on September 30, 1865. Edward returned to Kalamazoo and married Miss Sophia Bolden on April 20, 1869. A son, Fred, was born the following year. Edward supported the family by working as a barber and began to collect a veteran's pension on April 12, 1889. At some point after 1890, Edward left Kalamazoo and went to Detroit. He died at St. Mary's Hospital on February 1, 1911, of consumption (tuberculosis). He was buried at Forest Lawn Cemetery on February 3, 1911.

Stephen White was born about 1826 and, like Edward Kersey, was from Indiana. Not much is known about Stephen, except that his wife's name was Jane, and they had four children—two daughters, Mary and Jennie, and two sons, Henry and William. Stephen and his family resided in the village of Kalamazoo, and he worked as a day laborer. On October 10, 1863, Stephen enlisted at Kalamazoo in Company A, 102nd United States Colored Infantry, for a three-year period. He was promoted to corporal on December 1, 1864, and was discharged on September 30, 1865, at Charleston, South Carolina. Stephan returned to Kalamazoo but died in November 1882. He was buried at Potter's Field in Riverside Cemetery on November 11, 1882.

After the war, there was an influx of Black veterans to the Kalamazoo area. Perhaps Thomas Woodford or Rix Hammond had told their fellow soldiers of the opportunities available in the growing village. By the 1890s, a total of thirty-four Black veterans resided in Kalamazoo County. Many would come to Kalamazoo, marry and raise families. Twenty-two of these men had served with the 102nd USCT. Ten of the men were members of the local Post of the Grand Army of the Republic. The roster of veterans includes:

Ashberry Ash	Company A, 102nd USCT
James H. Bass	Company C, 102nd USCT
Nathan Beauregard	Company A, 102nd USCT
Edward L. Bennett	Company G, 102nd USCT
Creed Calloway	Company D, 102nd USCT
Gabriel Green (Samuel Allen)	102nd USCT (not assigned to a company)
Calvin Hackley	13th US Colored Artillery
Lovett Hammond	Company K, 102nd USCT
Rix Hammond	Company I, 102nd USCT

Elijah Harrison (Harris)	Company B, 102nd USCT
Spencer Hedges	Company E, 102nd USCT
George Henderson	Company E, 102nd USCT
Samuel Henderson	Company E, 102nd USCT
Jennings Hyatt	Company H, 116th USCT
James Jackson	Company C, 102nd USCT
Edward Kersey, first sergeant	Company C, 102nd USCT
George Mallory	Company E, 115th USCT
Achillies McCullough, corporal	Company A, 102nd USCT
Ellis McGerry	Company G, 55th Massachusetts Infantry
Alexander Morgan	Company G, 102nd USCT
George Morgan	Company C, 102nd USCT
Reuben Robbins	Company B, 25th USCT
Simeon Robbins	Company G, 55th Massachusetts Infantry
William H. Roberts	Company E, 24th USCT
William Riley Robinson	28th USCT (not assigned to a company)
Preston Scott	Company H, 102nd USCT
Edward Sheppard	Company I, 102nd USCT
Charles Simmons	Company B, 102nd USCT
William Henry Simmons, corporal	Company D, 102nd USCT
Richard Skipworth	Company E, 8th USCT
Benjamin F. Stewart	Company K, 15th USCT
Harrison H. Tillman	Company B, 102nd USCT
William Tucker	Company C, 102nd USCT
Albert Whaling (John Freeland)	5th US Colored Cavalry
Stephen White, corporal	Company A, 102nd USCT
Thomas Woodford, corporal	Company K, 102nd USCT

Albert Whaling, also known as John Freeland, lived in Kalamazoo after the war and died in 1934. He was the last Black Civil War veteran in Kalamazoo. Albert was interred at the Orcutt Post No. 79 lot in Riverside Cemetery.

6

The Homefront

Father is very busy just now making boots for the soldiers, he would go to see you, but if he stops, all hands in the shop would stop work.
—*Letter to Frank Hodgman from his mother, Frances, September 2, 1862*

The Ladies' Aid Society

The Ladies' Soldiers' Aid Society of Kalamazoo County was organized in 1861 to furnish soldiers from Kalamazoo County with basic needs that were either not met by the army or that were not readily available. Membership in the Ladies' Aid Society was open to any woman who wanted to aid the cause and included the wives, mothers and sisters of soldiers. They would knit socks, make shirts, bake pies and preserve various types of food to send to the boys in the field and, at times, would give assistance to the families of soldiers in need.

In 1862, Cornelia Stockbridge Sheldon was elected president of the society, Lucinda Hinsdale Stone as secretary and Ruth Webster as treasurer. In 1863, Ruth Potter was elected president, Cornelia Sheldon secretary and Ruth Webster continued as treasurer. These ladies served in their respective capacities until the close of the war. Interestingly, but not surprisingly, these women were also members of Kalamazoo's Ladies Library Association.

In 1863, the society organized a State Sanitary Fair to raise money for the care of the sick and wounded in the several military hospitals functioning around the country. This fair was to coincide with the annual Michigan State Agricultural Fair, held in Kalamazoo at the National Race Track grounds. It was recorded that the fair was "eminently successful."

In 1864, during the State Agricultural Fair, another sanitary fair opened in Kalamazoo on September 20 and ran for four days. The sanitary fair building that was erected especially for this event stood one hundred feet by sixty feet. It was designed to be temporary so that at the end of the fair the lumber used in its construction could be sold and the money placed in the fund. For a second time, it was held at the National Race Track.

The *Kalamazoo Telegraph* described the interior:

> *The profusion of evergreen trimmings makes the sight a beautiful one.... On either side of the building within wreaths of the same material are the names of the brave sons of America, who are the gallant leaders of our Army and Navy. Such names as Burnside, Grant, Meade, McClellan, Sherman, Siegel, Farragut and Porter stand forth in prominence....Exhibited on the west end of the hall, the battle-flags of Michigan regiments, tattered and torn, which give ample proof to the part borne by their followers on the battle-fields which have immortalized the names of Michigan soldiers. These, fourteen in number, were furnished for exhibition by the kindness and liberality of Adjutant General Robertson, as were also three Rebel stands of colors, taken as trophies in fair fight, and sent home to their friends by our soldiers as evidences of Michigan bravery and valor.*

The display of Michigan regimental battle flags generated the most interest among the visitors. Many comments were overheard, including, "My son fought under that flag," sometimes, sadly, followed by, "and he fell in battle."

Booths in the hall were set aside for each ladies' aid group from several other counties, including Wayne, Calhoun, Van Buren, Hillsdale, Allegan, Jackson, St. Clair and Lenawee. Many others participated, as well. At each booth, ladies displayed items to be sold to raise funds. Items such as paintings, quilts, animals, farm implements, musical instruments and many handmade objects were available for purchase, all donated for the event. Also within the hall was a booth that included a ballot box. For twenty-five cents, a patron could cast a straw ballot for president of the United States. The result of the election was 260 for Republican Abraham Lincoln, 116 for Democrat General George McClellan, two for Republican John C. Fremont and one for Confederate general Robert E. Lee.

The Homefront

Each of the four days saw thousands of Michiganders purchase tickets and walk through the gates. On Thursday, September 22, Michigan governor Austin Blair came from Lansing and addressed the crowds, thanking them for their continued support of the troops. His hour-long speech was well received by those in attendance. At the end of the four-day fair, the receipts were tallied, and $12,764.80 was raised. In 2020 dollars, that would equal $210,316.75.

The efforts of the society were not limited to the state fairs but went on year-round. In December 1863, the ladies publicly acknowledged "generous donations of fruits and vegetables" and listed funds collected in Pavilion and Brady Townships and the village of Climax, totaling $27.80. In 2020, that would equal $569.49.

Cornelia R. Stockbridge Sheldon was born in Bath, Maine, on December 18, 1827, to John and Eliza (Russell) Stockbridge. She married Theodore Pierce Sheldon of Kalamazoo between 1857 and 1860. Theodore's first wife, Hannah, died in 1857, leaving four daughters in the widower's care. Mr. Sheldon was a prominent banker in Kalamazoo, and Miss Stockbridge was a former schoolteacher in Allegan. Theodore and Cornelia had one daughter together, Cornelia, named for her mother. Mrs. Sheldon served as the president of the Ladies' Aid Society in 1862. Mr. Sheldon died in 1893, at the age of eighty-one. Cornelia died in Detroit after returning from a visit to Asheville, North Carolina. She was laid to rest at Mountain Home Cemetery next to her husband. Mrs. Sheldon's brother, Frances Brown Stockbridge, was a United States senator from Michigan, serving from 1887 to 1894.

Cornelia Stockbridge Sheldon. *Western Michigan University Archives.*

Mrs. Ruth Webster served as the treasurer for both the Ladies' Aid Society and the Ladies' Library, serving for twenty-four years in the latter position. She was also the librarian for fifteen years. She donated the land on Park Street to the Ladies' Library Association to erect its building in 1878. Ruth was married first to Daniel Thomas of Kalamazoo in 1841. A daughter, Julia, died at the age of fourteen. In 1848, Ruth married David Webster, a Kalamazoo attorney and later judge, who was born in

Ruth Webster. *Western Michigan University Archives.*

Charity Potter. *Western Michigan University Archives.*

1802 and died in 1860. Mrs. Webster was born in 1809 in New York and died in Kalamazoo in November 1878. The Websters are interred at Mountain Home Cemetery.

Charity Potter was born in Romulus, New York, in 1826. She was largely known as being devoted to community affairs. True to her name, Charity was involved in several charitable endeavors throughout her life. Her husband, Allen Potter, was born in New York in 1818. Allen and Charity came to Kalamazoo in 1845 from Lockport, New York. Previously, they had resided in Homer, Michigan, on the Chicago Road, (U.S. 12), where Allen worked in his father-in-law's hardware store. Mr. Potter established a hardware business in Kalamazoo and later served as vice president of the board of directors of the Michigan National Bank of Kalamazoo. After the incorporation of Kalamazoo as a city in 1884, Allen was elected as its first mayor. Charity passed away in 1921, at the age of ninety-four, outliving her husband by thirty-six years.

Ann Eliza (Champlin) Sill was born in New York in 1825 and died at her home at 328 Rose Street, Kalamazoo, on December 21, 1898. For many years, she was an active member of the Ladies' Library Association. Her husband, Dr. Joseph Sill, died in 1905, at the age of eighty-three. He was a practicing physician in Kalamazoo for over forty years. The Sills had no children.

Miss Mary Penfield, an early member and director of the Ladies' Aid Society, took it upon herself to do what she could to alleviate the pain and suffering of wounded soldiers. From 1862 to 1865, Mary served as a nurse, working in several military hospitals in places like Kentucky and Mississippi. Nurses during the war were looked on with the utmost gratitude by the soldiers. After returning to Kalamazoo at the close of the war, Mary served several years as the librarian for the Kalamazoo Ladies' Library. She never married. In the 1880s, the United States Congress was petitioned to provide a pension to Mary. It was approved, and she received twelve dollars per month for the rest of her life. Mary Penfield was born in New York in 1827 and died in Kalamazoo in 1897. She is also interred at Mountain Home.

The Draft

Nothing elicits fear to the core of a young man during wartime like the word *draft*. In Kalamazoo County it was no different. There was a draft ordered by the adjutant general of Michigan for the autumn of 1862; fortunately, there were sufficient volunteer enlistments to rescind that order. Another draft was ordered in the fall of 1863. This time there were not enough volunteers to prevent the dreaded occasion.

On October 27, 1863, the provost marshal of Kalamazoo, Captain Rollin C. Denison, and the board of enrollment met in the county courthouse to proceed with the task. The room was filled to capacity as excited spectators and nervous enrollees waited to hear the names called. The names of 6,123 eligible male citizens, all residents of Kalamazoo County, were written on slips of paper and placed in the wooden "Pandora's box." Measuring just twenty and a half inches by fifteen inches by eighteen inches, the box held the fate of Kalamazoo's young men.

According to *The 1880 History of Kalamazoo County*, forty-one names were drawn that night: James I. Graves, Thomas Pattison, Oliver Milham, Frank Hubbard, Jacob R. Campbell, Joseph Reego, Frank Marsala, Arnold Leys, George Ball, George W. Earl, John C. Bassett, Bradley Mills, John L. Phillips, Henry Wood, Rix Hammond, William Macomber, Joseph Quinn, Theodore R. Huntington, Stephen Hurd, James McCall, David B. Merrill, William H. Denman, Edward P. Titus, William Seelye, Patrick Rooney, Joseph Shellman, Henry E. Hoyt, Isaac Newton, Benjamin Russ, John H. Foquettte, Joseph Kensington, Aura James Burrell, George W. Coleman, James Agan, George L. Allen, George Young, William Heffron, Thomas Clarage, Jonathan Nickerson, Edwin H. Van Deusen and Solon S. Stanley.

The draft box. From this box, the names of eligible men were drawn to enter the service from Kalamazoo County. *Kalamazoo Valley Museum Collection.*

The following December, the *Kalamazoo Telegraph* ran an article explaining how one could be exempted from service:

- *If one was the only son of elderly or invalid parents, or those parents could request exemption on the same basis;*
- *A parent could request one of their sons exempted;*
- *The only brother of a dependent sibling;*
- *That two or more members of the family are already serving in the military;*
- *That the person is the father of motherless children, under the age of 12 years;*
- *Or that the person is under 20 years of age, over the age of 35 and married, or, over the age of 45.*

The draftee could also obtain a certificate of disability from a doctor or surgeon sworn before a judge or magistrate. The doctor "must be a graduate of the medical school or college, and a respectable practitioner." In other words, no quacks or snake oil salesmen.

The Homefront

According to the records of the adjutant general of the state of Michigan, the following men were the draftees who served in the war:

Kalamazoo Township:
Hiram Comstock	Company G, 4th Michigan Cavalry (attributed to Allegan County)
Rix Hammond	Company F, 2nd Michigan Cavalry
Albert W. Hungerford	102nd United States Colored Infantry*
Bradley Mills	Company I, 4th Michigan Cavalry
James F. O'Conner	4th Michigan Cavalry*
Charles H. Olmstead	Company H, 2nd Michigan Cavalry
John Wright	Company B, 4th Michigan Cavalry

Climax Township:
William B. Chandler	Company B, 2nd Michigan Cavalry
William Clipperton	4th Michigan Cavalry*
Hubbard Steadman	Corporal, Company L, 2nd Michigan Cavalry
Nathanial Vaughn	Company L, 2nd Michigan Cavalry
John C. Williams	2nd Michigan Cavalry*
Elias Worden	Company M, 2nd Michigan Cavalry

Texas Township:
Amos Welch	Company M, 2nd Michigan Cavalry

Comstock:
Charles Dunn	Company C, 2nd Michigan Cavalry

Charleston Township:
Edward Coe	Company M, 2nd Michigan Cavalry
James Riley	Company I, 2nd Michigan Cavalry
John Galligan	Company I, 2nd Michigan Cavalry

Pavilion Township:
Nathan E. Harrison	Company M, 4th Michigan Cavalry

Portage Township:
William Koster	Company A, 2nd Michigan Cavalry

Prairie Rhonde:
William A. Cox	Company M, 2nd Michigan Cavalry

*Not assigned to a specific company in the regiment.

Rix Hammond was mustered into Company F, 2nd Michigan Cavalry on October 28, 1863. He was transferred on May 31, 1865, to Company I, 102nd United States Colored Troops and was discharged on September 30, 1865. This situation is unique, as Rix Hammond was Black. There are only a few known Michigan men of color who served in otherwise all-White regiments. Another was Aquila Lett, a resident of Paw Paw, Michigan, who served in Company K, 13th Michigan Infantry from September 1864 to June 1865.

John H. Foquette (Foquett), one of the eligible citizens, had previously served in Company D, 17th Michigan Infantry. He enlisted on August 4, 1862, at the age of eighteen, and was discharged for disability in April 1863, due to wounds received in the Battle of South Mountain, Maryland, on September 14, 1862. Due to this previous service, he was not required to reenter the army.

Another draft was held on March 15, 1865, when ninety-seven names were drawn. Of these, eight were accepted into the service.

Kalamazoo:

Frederick Dall	15th Michigan Infantry*
George Fleck	Company C, 15th Michigan Infantry
Squire Lampman	Company K, 14th Michigan Infantry
John March	Company I, 15th Michigan Infantry
Michael McGuire	Company E, 16th Michigan Infantry

Texas Township:

Cyrenias Sadler	Company D, 15th Michigan Infantry

Wakeshma Township:

Theodore Clark	Company G, 15th Michigan Infantry

Brady Township:

Herschal Foster	Company I, 16th Michigan Infantry

*Not assigned to a specific company in the regiment.

Herschal Foster previously served in Company G, 13th Michigan Infantry. He enlisted on October 11, 1861, and was discharged for disability on February 7, 1863.

The Homefront

The *Telegraph* also ran an advertisement in the same issue, stating, "Substitutes for drafted men can be obtained upon application to John Albertson, Esq., *Telegraph* Printing office." It would appear that attorney Albertson was in the business of obtaining substitutes for a price, perhaps a lucrative business in the early 1860s.

7

The War Ends

Spontaneous, Individual Explosion

On Sunday, April 2, 1865, the news of the fall of Richmond, Virginia, the capital of the Confederacy, was greeted throughout the North with great excitement. Thirty-one years later, Captain Charles May, formerly of the 2nd Michigan Infantry, wrote of his memory of the occasion:

> Here in Michigan it was a warm, genial April morning and we got the news by 9 o'clock. Men filled the streets with excited, beaming faces, they shook hands with each other, the news spread from house to house. "Richmond has fallen." "Our army is in its streets." "The flag is waving over the rebel capital." "Lincoln is there—the city is on fire and our soldiers are fighting the flames!!"
>
> All day the good news spread through the town and throughout the country, far and wide; no business was done, the happiness was universal and supreme. When night came the whole population, with half the county besides, it seemed to me, was in the streets. Bonfires of tar barrels, dry goods boxes and other combustible materials were lit and the whole heavens were illuminated with the brightness of day. From the balcony, or iron railing, then in front of William B. Clark's store on Main Street, where I was called to speak, was witnessed such a scene as was never presented to me before and can never be again. Talk about crowds—about enthusiasm!

The War Ends

Kalamazoo was not half as large then as it is today, but from Court House square to the Kalamazoo House and Portage Street was one dense solid mass of humanity, excited and thrilled as only men can be by a crowning victory at the end of a great, four years' war.

In the following days, all of Kalamazoo and the surrounding villages would watch for any news of Grant's pursuit of the rebel forces under Robert E. Lee. The Union army finally caught up with Lee at Saylor's (Sailor's) Creek and then at Mr. Wilmer McLean's parlor at Appomattox Court House. Captain May continued:

It was the 9th of April, less than a week after the fall of Richmond. The scenes that now occurred here in Kalamazoo, in Michigan, all through the north beg description. Great as was the excitement and the joy over Richmond, there was some repose, some self control, some attempt at an orderly and concerted expression of the public feeling. But now pandemonium was let loose. There was no order, no reserve, no self control. The excitement, so to speak, took the form of spontaneous, individual explosion. Sober citizens yelled and shouted like wild men; they ran about the streets, they embraced and hugged each other like girls. As under ether or laughing gas each man showed out under that excitement his own nature. Some wept, some laughed; men and boys ran shouting through the streets or rode horses or donkeys up and down, ringing bells or blowing horns. Some rushed into saloons to treat and to drink; others tried to drag men up to public bars who were never seen there. But in all this wild excitement there were, of course, sober, patriotic citizens who did not indulge in these grotesque extravagances or seek to blunt or drown their senses in drink, but with hearts full of joy and gratitude, thanked God in their homes or offices all that day for this great victory—that now at last this wicked rebellion was crushed, the majesty and power of the government vindicated, and slavery, the hateful and barbarous institution, the cause of all the trouble, wiped out forever.

Many families in not only Kalamazoo, but in Climax, Schoolcraft, Richland and Galesburg greeted the news with thoughts of their loved ones that would be coming home soon. Many others were both joyous and saddened, for their father, son or brother would not be returning to them.

And then the blessed thought, too, that there would be no more bloodshed, no more precious lives lost, but white winged peace would again cover the land and grim visage war, with all his long train of horrors, retire before the glad opening of the spring.

A Convulsive Shudder

On Friday, April 14, Good Friday in the Christian tradition, life went quietly on as usual, except for the overlying happiness due to the cessation of hostilities between the North and the South. The atmosphere in Kalamazoo was cheerful and optimistic. In twenty-four hours, that cheerful optimism would become anguish and incredulity.

It was the morning of Saturday, April 15, that the news of Lincoln's assassination reached Kalamazoo by telegraph. Captain Charles May again wrote of his observations, this time as to the village's anguished reaction:

> *On the way to my office that morning as I was passing through the park, [Bronson Park], an excited neighbor met me with the exclamation, "Awful news—Lincoln and Seward both assassinated!" I can go to the spot within a foot where I then stood transfixed—and how strange that it should have been within twenty feet of where Abraham Lincoln stood where he delivered that speech in the park....A few moments later I was down town where the streets at that early hour, were already full of people. There was no noise, no outcry, no running to and fro. Men seemed crushed by the news—their faces blanched, their voices hollow. Here and there would be a ripple of outward excitement as some rebel sympathizer who had unguardedly expressed his delight was set upon by the indignant crowd. When Mr. Stanton's first dispatch was read saying that there was no hope, and his last announcing in briefest, saddest words the presidents' death, a convulsive shudder ran through the multitude and an awful grown, a sound of pain, was heard which words cannot describe.*

Captain May continued, saying that while the residents were in a state of disbelief, there were no public announcements or formal statements made by village officials. There were many people in the streets, their numbers increasing as the day went by, yet there was no unified outpouring of grief. Each person seemed to hold their sorrow inward. Another underlying concern was the distinct possibility that there would be more horrifying news to come out of Washington. Captain May continued:

> *But all day the bells tolled sadly in the steeples—the bells that only yesterday, as it were, had pealed forth their glad and thrilling chimes over the nation's great victory. But towards evening, some men, and especially many women, bethought themselves that tomorrow would be Sunday and*

> the stores were soon rid of their stock of velvet and crape and busy hands that afternoon draped all the churches, pulpit and altar and walls, outside and in the public buildings and places of business were also hung in mourning. Every private house, too, was draped in some fashion, as though it contained its own beloved dead. The whole land was clothed in funeral black that Sunday afternoon and on the morrow all the loyal churches in the loyal north were in deepest mourning emblems and filled with solemn, mourning congregations.

In the several days following, the people of Kalamazoo were eager for any additional news or updates on the continuing drama in the nation's capital. Accounts of the ceremonies taking place in major cities around the country were repeated in the *Kalamazoo Daily Telegraph* and the *Kalamazoo Gazette*: "For days the great lamination went on as the people turned their eyes towards Washington and eagerly read every particular of the awful tragedy. The press, too, from every quarter brought the news of tolling bells, of mourning cities, of weeping multitudes, and a thousand teeming tributes of honor and affection. Never in the history of the world had a whole people been so moved and affected—no, not when Washington died, for he died peacefully in his bed, and besides he was not loved like Lincoln."

On April 21, 1865, Lincoln's remains left Washington bound for Springfield, Illinois, traveling through seven states, including Maryland, Pennsylvania, New Jersey, New York, Ohio, Indiana and finally to Illinois. At several towns and cities, Lincoln's casket was viewed by hundreds of thousands of mourners. Many places that the train did not pass through, like Kalamazoo, held their own memorial observances:

> What transpired here, in our own midst, was only a sample of what was felt and done by twenty millions of people. It was arranged that on the day the funeral train of the martyred president should start from the nation's capital for that long and wonderful journey of triumphant sorrow across the continent the whole people should flock to their churches and join together in solemn funeral observances. I remember that day, the 21st of April, 1865, as distinctly as though it were yesterday. That whole month of April had been unusually mild and genial and this day, here in Michigan, at least was one of the mildest, but as if in keeping with the solemn services of the occasion the sky was overcast and a soft, gentle spring rain fell from the weeping clouds.

For Gallantry in Action

It's just a small cemetery. Very quiet and peaceful. The occasional car drives by. Not many who know of this cemetery realize that a Medal of Honor recipient is buried there. Liberty Street Cemetery, located on G Avenue in Alamo Township, has a little more than three hundred occupants. One of those in permanent residence is Elliott Malloy Norton.

Elliott Norton was born in Connecticut on June 15, 1834. When he was young, the Norton family made their way to Michigan, settling in Wayland, Allegan County. In 1862, Elliott enlisted in company B, 6th Michigan Cavalry at Grand Rapids. The 6th was part of the famous Michigan Cavalry Brigade, which also included the 1st, 5th, 6th and 7th Michigan Cavalry Regiments, as well as Battery M, 2nd United States Light Artillery.

Norton was promoted to sergeant on April 1, 1863, just three months before the pivotal Battle of Gettysburg, and then to sergeant major on August 6, 1864. On that same date, Elliott was discharged as an enlisted man, only to be mustered as a second lieutenant.

In the closing days of the war, the Union army of the Potomac cornered the remnants of Robert E. Lee's Confederate army of Northern Virginia at Sailor's Creek, near Farmville, Virginia. On April 6, 1865, during the ensuing action, Elliott captured a Confederate battle flag. For his action that day, he was recommended for and later received the Congressional Medal of Honor.

Elliott described his experience:

> *It was near the last gasp of the war, only a day or two before Lee's surrender—Sailor's Creek, it was called. The battle began about half past three o'clock in the afternoon. I was then a lieutenant and acting adjutant of my regiment. At five-thirty we were pursuing the enemy in "columns of fours" at a gallop. I was riding at the head of the regiment with the colonel. Seeing a squad of the enemy, about twenty in number, about sixty rods to the left with a battle flag, I left the regiment and went for them, with no other object than to capture the flag. I had made several attempts to do this before but failed. When within six or eight rods* [one rod equals 16.5 feet] *of the party they fired together at me, leaving their carbines empty and me unharmed. With drawn sabre, I rushed upon them and ordered them to throw down their arms which they did. They did not so quickly give up the flag. But I suppose they saw I was bound to have it and as some of our troops were now ahead of these Confederates they sullenly resigned the flag*

The War Ends

to my care. Tearing it from its staff and thrusting it inside my coat, I told my prisoners to fall in line and start for the rear.

It was after seven o'clock that evening when I overtook the command, then going into camp. I kept my prize secret until evening, when as we (the colonel and I occupied the same tent) were about turning in I told Col. Vinton that if he would promise not to say anything, I would show him something. He agreed and I then pulled out my trophy. The old war-dog fairly danced with delight. "Jeems River!" cried he, "my regiment shall have the honor of capturing that flag. No, Adjutant, I shall break faith with you!" And he did. But I forgave him.

After the surrender, I was ordered to Washington in company with a number of other flag-captors, to turn over to the Secretary of War all the flags captured by the cavalry corps. Here we each received a furlough of thirty days and a Medal of Honor. My battle flag belonged to the 44th Tennessee Regiment. It was of heavy silk, 12x4½ feet in dimensions, with gilt stars and bars, and the motto, "Death to Invaders."

Elliott returned to his regiment following his thirty-day furlough. He was transferred to the 1st Michigan Cavalry in November 1865 and spent four months on duty in the Utah Territory. He was discharged from the army at Salt Lake City on March 10, 1866.

After his discharge, Elliott came home to Michigan and resumed his vocation of farming. In 1868, he married Lucy Bennett, a native of the village of Schoolcraft. The United States Census of 1870 shows Elliott and Lucy residing in Cooper Township. By 1880, they removed to Grand Rapids, and most of their nine children were born there. When Elliott died in 1899, at the age of sixty-four, the Norton family was living in North Shade Township in Gratiot County.

Elliott and Lucy are buried together with three of their children, Max, Effie and Abbie, at Liberty Street Cemetery.

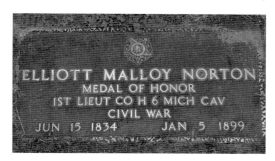

Plaque on the grave of Lieutenant Elliott Norton, Liberty Street Cemetery. *Photo by the author.*

8

THE POSTWAR YEARS

OUR VERY OWN REBEL

He survived the hardest fighting at Fort Donelson in February 1862. He endured several months as a prisoner of war at Camp Douglas, just outside of Chicago. What almost killed him was pulling a tooth.

Burr Bannister was born in October 1836, in Brockport, New York. Beginning in 1855, he spent some time in Kalamazoo before finding his way south to Shelbyville, Tennessee. Arriving there, he studied dentistry and set up a practice in neighboring Richmond, a small community just eleven miles southwest. He became enamored with the southern way of life and made many friends.

When the Civil War came, Burr sided with the secessionists of West Tennessee. He enlisted in 1861 at the age of twenty-four years, joining Captain Thomas K. Porter's 2nd Tennessee Field Battery and was promoted to orderly sergeant. Surely, Burr looked the part in his gray frock coat with red collar (denoting the artillery branch of the army) and a blue model 1847 army forage cap.

In February 1862, he found himself at Fort Donelson near Dover, Tennessee, on the western shore of the Cumberland River. On February 14, Union gunboats attacked the Confederate fort to gain control of the waterway. The Union and Confederate cannons dueled for an hour and a half, leaving the Yankee vessels crippled and their commanding officer wounded. In the next several days, General Ulysses S. Grant would dislodge

The Postwar Years

the hold the rebels had, freeing the river and enabling the Federal forces to occupy Kentucky and West Tennessee.

In 1909, Burr recalled the fight at Fort Donelson: "Our company went into the battle one hundred and sixty-three strong. The second day fifty-four answered at roll-call, and after the surrender [of Fort Donelson]. I could find but fourteen to answer. I suppose some may have been rounded up in other commands. We were sent to Camp Douglas, near Chicago, and held there eight months and five days. The experience of prison life might fill a large volume."

Evidently, Burr became disillusioned with army life and the Southern cause, because, most likely after his release from Camp Douglas, he returned to Kalamazoo in 1863 and set up a new practice at 117 Main Street. He married Miss Lucy Anderson, and in 1866, their first son, Guy, was born. A second son, Walter, was born in 1870.

In 1867, Burr and an associate, George F. Green, were awarded a patent by the U.S. Patent Office, for an Automatic Tooth Plugger. The description of the patent includes an "engine operated by means of compressed air" and a spring and a piston rod.

Apparently, dentistry was not as lucrative an occupation as Burr had hoped. He opened the Kalamazoo Emery Wheel Company, which manufactured grinding and polishing wheels. In April 1874, he and John C. Perkins were awarded a patent for a polishing and grinding wheel. They assigned one third of the rights to William H. Stoddart, also of the village. The business flourished, and Burr became a prominent citizen in Kalamazoo. He joined the local Masonic Lodge, helped to fund the new opera house in 1881, was a member of the Kalamazoo Humane Society and was made the assistant marshal for the 1889 Independence Day parade.

Still practicing dentistry at the age of seventy-five, Burr probably never imagined that a tooth would be his nemesis. In the September 26, 1911 edition of the *Kalamazoo Telegraph-Press*, the following account was provided: "Dr. Bannister was extracting a tooth when the dental chair toppled and partially fell, striking him and pinning him to the floor. The force of the blow was sufficient to cause internal hemorrhages. He was taken to Bronson hospital.... For a time after the accident it was thought his injuries would prove fatal."

Burr underwent surgery performed by Dr. Rush McNair. A few days later, Dr. Bannister was able to eat and showed improvement.

On June 24, 1916, Dr. Burr Bannister was found at home, dead in his bed. The coroner determined that a stroke, commonly referred to as apoplexy, was the cause. Burr was seventy-nine years old. He was buried next to his wife, Lucy, at Mountain Home Cemetery.

Kalamazoo's Claim on Memorial Day

Over the last several years, there has been a debate over the origin of the tradition of decorating the graves of fallen soldiers with flowers in the United States. There are some who say it was started in Charleston, South Carolina, on May 1, 1865, by former slaves. Others claim that Confederate women began honoring the rebel soldiers in Richmond, Virginia, on May 31, 1866. In 1968, the United States Congress recognized Waterloo, New York, as the birthplace of Memorial Day, with its documented observance on May 5, 1866. The Center for Civil War Research, located at the University of Mississippi, recognizes an observance even earlier. Kalamazoo can, somewhat, claim that honor.

Although the first simple act of decorating the graves did not actually take place in Kalamazoo, or even in Michigan, it was three women and a young girl, three from Kalamazoo and one from Hudson, Michigan, who decorated soldiers' graves with flowers at Arlington Heights, Virginia, on April 13, 1862.

The Reverend Franklin W. May was the chaplain of the 2nd Michigan Infantry. His brother Dwight was the captain of Company I and his other brother Charles was the captain of Company K. As an officer, Frank was allowed to bring his family along, including his wife, Maria, and their two daughters, Josephine, also known as Josie, age fourteen, and little Ella, age two. Maria, Josie and Ella decorated the graves, along with Sarah Evans, the wife of Sergeant George H. Evans of Company B.

Maria, Josephine and Sarah acted as unofficial Army nurses. Whenever a soldier was wounded or ill, the ladies were by his side. While the 2nd Michigan Infantry was on duty in Washington, D.C., in the spring of 1862, Josephine and Ella walked the grounds of Arlington, the home of Confederate general Robert E. Lee. Mrs. Lee's rose garden had been turned into a cemetery for the Union dead from the First Battle of Bull Run in nearby Manassas, Virginia. Josephine knew that some of the graves belonged to members of the 2nd Michigan, so she and Ella gathered flowers and placed them on their graves. Telling Mrs. May and Mrs. Evans of the decorating of the graves, they, too, joined in the task. Soon, all the bare graves were adorned with flowers.

In November 1862, the 2nd Michigan was transferred from the 3rd Corps to the 9th Corps, Army of the Potomac. As such, the 2nd was soon on its way south and, on December 12, crossed the Rappahannock River during the Battle of Fredericksburg. The Michigan boys were held in reserve but still sustained casualties due to the enemy shelling by artillery. The following

The Postwar Years

spring, the May family and Mrs. Evans once again decorated the graves of the soldiers buried at Fredericksburg. These graves would eventually be part of the Fredericksburg National Cemetery.

When the war ended, the May family returned to Kalamazoo. Josephine never married and died at the age of twenty-five in 1872. Maria passed away in 1876, and Frank lived until 1880. Ella married Joseph S. Wilson, and the couple moved to Spokane, Washington. Ella died in 1901, at the age of forty-one. Joseph died in 1925. All are buried at the May family plot, in Section 103 of Mountain Home Cemetery. For many years following the war, Josephine and Maria's graves were decorated on Memorial Day. The local veterans recognized their service as army nurses, even if the State of Michigan or federal government did not.

Sarah and George Evans left Kalamazoo after the war and moved to Des Moines, Iowa. George joined Crocker Post No. 12 of the Grand Army of the Republic. In 1883, the comrades of Post No. 12 voted to recognize Sarah's contribution to the tradition of Memorial Day and made her an honorary member. A few months later, they did the same for Ella, even though she was just a small child during the war.

Sarah died in 1884 at the age of forty-two. She and her husband, George, are buried at Woodland Cemetery in Des Moines.

In the February 21, 1884 edition of the *National Tribune*, published in Washington, D.C., the following article appeared:

> *The Mother of Memorial Day*
> *On February 1 death entered our camp and mustered out of our ranks Mrs. Sarah Nicholas Evans, an honorary member of Crocker Post No. 12. When, early in 1861, her husband, Comrade George H. Evans, responded to President Lincoln's call for 75,000 men, and enlisted in the 2nd Michigan infantry volunteers, she accompanied him to the front, and for three years and nine months served in camp, upon the battlefield, and in hospital.... Mrs. Evans was one of the four ladies with whom the observance originated of what has since become our National Memorial Day.*
>
> *On the 13th of April, just one year after the fall of Fort Sumter, she, with Mrs. May, wife of the chaplain of the regiment, and her two daughters, Josie and Ella, gathered wild flowers and strewed them upon the graves of those who had been their schoolmates and neighbors at home. But they did not stop there, but continued their sublime work until the graves of all the heroic dead then at Arlington had been decked by the loving hands of these noble women.*

The debate will still continue about who began the tradition of decorating the graves of soldiers with flowers in the springtime, but it was eventually the Grand Army of the Republic that formalized the observance to be held on May 30, 1868, and continue each year, "while a survivor of the war remains to honor the memory of his departed comrades."

The Murder of Sheriff Benjamin F. Orcutt

Benjamin Franklin Orcutt was born in Vermont in 1815. He came to Kalamazoo in 1836 and was elected constable five years later. Orcutt was also, for several years, a deputy United States marshal. He served in the Mexican-American War of 1846 as first sergeant of Company A, 1st Michigan Volunteers, under Captain Fredrick W. Curtenius, also of Kalamazoo. During the Civil War, Benjamin Orcutt was commissioned lieutenant colonel of the 25th Michigan Infantry in 1862.

On December 12, 1867, he died of wounds received while pursuing men who attempted to break prisoners out of jail. In the early morning hours of December 3, Sheriff Orcutt was woken by noises coming from outside the jail. At that time, the jail stood on the east end of Bronson Park, facing Rose Street. It was a two-story, poorly constructed wooden building with the living quarters for the sheriff and his family on the ground floor and the prisoner's cells on the second floor. Orcutt pulled on his clothes, grabbed his revolver and ran outside.

There were two men trying to break out the prisoners on the second floor, and when Orcutt came around the corner of the building, the two men took off. The sheriff, thinking that the two were escaped prisoners, ordered them to halt. One headed toward the corner of Michigan Avenue and Rose Street, crossing to the opposite corner. That is the one that the sheriff chased, firing his revolver as he ran. The man ran down an ally to about where the lobby of the Radison Plaza Hotel is today. There was a brick building on the corner facing Michigan, an ally to the right and then another building, Bartlett's Bookstore. In the ally was a large burr oak tree. The man was hiding behind that tree when Sheriff Orcutt came into the ally. Shots were fired, and Orcutt was hit.

He stumbled back to the jail, and his wife asked, "Did you kill them?"

Orcutt replied, "No, but I think he has killed me." Colonel Orcutt had been shot through the shoulder. He died eleven days later. The prisoners

The Postwar Years

Lieutenant Colonel Benjamin F. Orcutt. From a wartime photograph. *Kalamazoo Valley Museum Collection.*

were still in jail. One of the two men, Gus Shaw, also known as Stephen Boyle, was caught in New York City the following February.

After Sheriff Orcutt's death, several prominent residents, mostly Civil War veterans, gathered and planned the funeral, which was attended by a great many residents of the village and surrounding area. The expenses were paid by the county. With her husband dead, Emily Orcutt and her children had to eke out an existence. In October 1869, the Kalamazoo County Board of Supervisors debated implementing a tax to raise $2,000 as a pension for the late sheriff's family. This was voted down. The board then took up a proposal to raise $1,000 for the Orcutts. The vote was a tie, so it, too, did not pass. There is no indication that the matter was ever taken up again.

In the fall of 1871, a rumor was circulating in the village that the county had paid the mortgage on the Orcutt's home. Many in the community would express their delight to the family at this turn of events. Unfortunately, this rumor was not true. In a letter to the editor of the *Kalamazoo Daily Telegraph*, Emily explained and expressed her frustration about the issue, stating that the family had never received "one cent" from the village or the county since Colonel Orcutt was buried. For the

Orcutt Monument, Orcutt family plot, Mountain Home Cemetery. *Photo by the author.*

rest of her life, Emily worked as a seamstress to provide for herself and for the children.

The large, white marble memorial standing on the Orcutt family lot in Mountain Home Cemetery was given as a tribute by the citizens of

The Postwar Years

Kalamazoo. It was erected in 1872. The front bears a shield with the name Orcutt. The three other sides are inscribed:

> *Lieut. Col. B.F. Orcutt, 25th Mich. Vol. Inf'ty, War of 1861, Died 1867, AE 53.*
> *In War a Soldier, In Peace, the Citizens Guardian.*
> *Erected by His Fellow Citizens, as a Token of Regard.*

THE VETERANS ORGANIZE

At the close of the Civil War, many veterans' organizations were formed. The one that still survives today has its origins in the horror that was the assassination of President Lincoln. On the night of April 15, 1865, a group of army officers gathered to plan a defense for the possible overthrow of the federal government. A few days later, another meeting of veterans was held in Philadelphia to pledge allegiance to the Union and to plan for participation in the funeral arrangements. These officers, who served as an honor guard for President Lincoln's funeral cortege, met again on May 31, 1865, and established a permanent organization called the Military Order of the Loyal Legion of the United States. This organization included the commissioned officers of the Union army and navy, much like the Society of the Cincinnati from the American Revolution, and continues today with their blood descendants.

The spring of 1865 saw several other veterans' organizations created, including the Societies of the Army of the James, Army of the Potomac, Army of the Cumberland, the Sultana Survivors and Prisoners of War. And then there are the regimental organizations. The list goes on and on.

On the night of April 6, 1866, a small group of thirteen Union veterans gathered in the upstairs rooms of a building in Decatur, Illinois, and formed an organization that would shape the destiny of our country for the next sixty years.

They were led by Major Benjamin Franklin Stephenson, former surgeon of the 14th Illinois Infantry. The Grand Army of the Republic (GAR) was the first nationwide veteran's organization in the United States. Major Stephenson's vision was an organization that would bring together the soldiers and sailors who had forged bonds of friendship in the struggles of the war. Membership was restricted to veterans who were of good moral

Membership badge of the Grand Army of the Republic. *Courtesy of Sons of Union Veterans of the Civil War.*

Bronze lapel button, official recognition button of the Grand Army of the Republic. *From the author's collection; photo by Michael B. Culp.*

character, possessed an honorable discharge and had never born arms against the United States.

One of the organization's underlying doctrines was that all veterans would be eligible for membership, regardless of race or skin color. The Grand Army of the Republic has the distinction of being the only social organization of the nineteenth and early twentieth centuries to allow Black men and Native Americans as full and equal members.

In 1905, the commander of the Department of Arkansas said it best: "I love the GAR. When I meet a man wearing the GAR button, I do not stop to see if he is dressed in broadcloth or if he has a pair of overalls, neither do I care whether he is black or white. I only see in back of the button a man who had the courage to enlist as a soldier and risk his life in defense of our glorious country."

Posts were organized when there was a group of ten or more veterans who applied for a charter. Generally, only one post could be organized per village or city. However, more posts could be organized if there was a large enough population to sustain the additional posts. For example, Detroit had seven—Fairbanks Post No. 17, Farquhar Post No. 162, John Brown Post No. 184, Detroit Post No. 384, Michigan Post No. 393, John C. Freemont Post No. 406 and O.M. Poe Post No. 433. All of the members of Post No. 184, as it was located in a primarily Black neighborhood, were United States Colored Troops veterans.

Posts would generally meet on a weekly basis. Veterans applied for membership to a local post that would vote on the application by using the ballot box and marble system. A white ball was an affirmative vote, but if three black balls were cast during the voting, the candidate was not accepted, hence the term "being blackballed." Once a veteran was admitted to membership, he was referred to as "comrade." Incidentally, there were a few posts in various places across the country made entirely of navy veterans. They referred to each other as "shipmate."

Many posts built their own memorial hall to hold meetings. On one wall of the post room, there would be a rack of muskets. These would eventually be used to fire a salute at the funeral of a deceased comrade or during Memorial Day ceremonies. In the early years, however, the muskets were there for a different reason.

In the years immediately following the war, the threat of the South renewing hostilities was a very real fear in the North. Today, we think of the slogan "the South will rise again" almost as a punch line. There was nothing humorous about it in the 1860s and 1870s. The Grand Army saw itself as the defenders of the nation, and the veterans wanted to be ready in case they were needed again.

The officers of a post consisted of a commander, senior and junior vice commanders, an adjutant who functioned as a secretary and the quartermaster, or treasurer. Additionally, there was a color bearer, chaplain, officer of the day, guard, patriotic instructor and a post surgeon. This position was very important. Most often, the post surgeon was a former army doctor or even a hospital steward. He was expected to treat the members of the post for free. Most posts would set aside time in their meetings to change each other's bandages on wounds that had never healed.

All of the posts in one or more states constituted a department, as in the Department of Michigan. An annual meeting of the representatives of each post elected officers to act as the administration at the state level at the state convention or Department Encampment. Reports of the various officers would be presented, proposed changes to the bylaws would be debated and voted on and a new slate of officers for the ensuing term would be elected. The delegates of the Department Encampment would also elect delegates to represent the department at the annual national convention, called the National Encampment. National Encampments were held each year in various major cities around the country. Some cities were chosen to host encampments multiple times, like Indianapolis, Indiana; Grand Rapids, Michigan; Cleveland, Ohio; and Buffalo, New York. New officers would be chosen to direct the organization and set policy for the ensuing term. The most prominent elected position was the commander-in-chief. The encampments would last an entire week, and the grand parade would usually be held on Wednesday. Businesses would close, and schools would let the children out early so that all could witness the grand spectacle that was the masses of veterans marching through the city. The veterans would march with their flags flying and fife and drum corps playing the old wartime songs from the Civil War.

In the early days, the encampments were just that—massive tent cities were erected, and the veterans were lodged there. In later years, as the veterans aged, they preferred the comforts of hotels. Some families residing in the host cities opened their homes to the veterans, because there just was not enough hotel space to accommodate the thousands of visitors to the encampment. It has been recorded that in the 1890s there were so many visitors to the encampments that the population of the host city would actually double. It was not uncommon for thousands of members of the Grand Army to attend, regardless of whether they were official delegates to the convention. The numbers increased as the other organizations affiliated with the GAR held their conventions at the same time and place, including their Auxiliary, the Woman's Relief Corps, the Sons of Veterans, the Ladies' Aid Society, Auxiliary to the Sons of Veterans, the Daughters of Veterans and the Ladies of the Grand Army of the Republic. These affiliated organizations made up the official Grand Army Family.

The GAR, at its zenith in 1890, reached 409,400 members and over ten thousand posts. By 1954, there was just one veteran left. Albert Woolson, of Duluth, Minnesota, was a drummer boy in the 1st Minnesota Heavy Artillery. He died in August 1956 at the age of 109.

The Grand Army's cardinal principles were fraternity, charity and loyalty. Fraternity referred to the comradeship of all veterans who fought to preserve the Union. Their gatherings would "foster those fraternal feelings born upon the battlefield." Charity referred to taking care of those disabled veterans who could not care for themselves, due to wounds or loss of limb, and caring for the widows and orphans of those who did not return. Loyalty referred to defending the Union if again called to do so, as well as teaching and being a role model of patriotism and honoring the flag of the United States of America for all it represents.

Although the GAR was organized to be nonsectarian and nonpolitical, it eventually held a considerable amount of political power. Across the North, governors, state legislators and members of Congress were former soldiers. Five of its members would eventually become president of the United States: Ulysses S. Grant, Rutherford B. Hayes, James A. Garfield, Benjamin Harrison and William McKinley. It was said that you "couldn't get elected dog catcher unless you had the backing of the Grand Army of the Republic."

The Postwar Years

The veterans of the Grand Army used their newfound political clout in several ways. United States senator John A. Logan of Illinois, a former major general, served three consecutive terms as the commander-in-chief of the GAR, from 1868 to 1871. His impassioned oratory and persuasive debate, which included what was referred to as "waving the bloody shirt," was responsible for Congress passing laws creating expanded pensions for disabled veterans and their widows and minor children. Additionally, the official designation of Flag Day, the flying of flags in front of schools and in classrooms and students reciting the Pledge of Allegiance at the beginning of the school day, are all results of the efforts of the GAR. Its legacy also includes several Civil War battlefield parks that are part of the National Park Service, including Gettysburg, Antietam, Manassas and Vicksburg.

At the time of the Civil War, there was no Veterans' Administration. There were no Veterans' Homes or VA hospitals. It was the Grand Army of the Republic that spearheaded the efforts to establish Soldiers' Homes in places like Grand Rapids, Michigan; Milwaukee, Wisconsin; Lincoln, Nebraska; and Chelsea, Massachusetts.

Memorial Day

During his administration as commander-in-chief, Logan designated May 30, 1868, to be the first coordinated, nationwide observance of Memorial Day. It was a day that was set aside to decorate the graves of those who died defending the Union. It was referred to by the veterans as their "Holy Day."

To ensure that veterans would observe the same day, Logan issued General Order No. 11, which states:

Headquarters, Grand Army of the Republic
Washington, D.C.
May 5, 1868

The 30th day of May, 1868, is designated for the purpose of strewing with flowers or otherwise decorating the graves of comrades who died in defense of their country during the late rebellion, and whose bodies now lie in almost every city, village, and hamlet church-yard in the land. In this observance no form of ceremony is prescribed, but posts and comrades will in their own way arrange such fitting services and testimonials of respect as circumstances may permit.

We are organized, comrades, as our regulations tell us, for the purpose, among other things, "of preserving and strengthening those kind and fraternal feelings which have bound together the soldiers, sailors, and marines who united to suppress the late rebellion." What can aid more to assure this result than cherishing tenderly the memory of our heroic dead, who made their breasts a barricade between our country and its foes? Their soldier lives were the reveille of freedom to a race in chains, and their deaths the tattoo of rebellious tyranny in arms. We should guard their graves with sacred vigilance. All that the consecrated wealth and taste of the nation can add to their adornment and security is but a fitting tribute to the memory of her slain defenders. Let no wanton foot tread rudely on such hallowed grounds. Let pleasant paths invite the coming and going of reverent visitors and fond mourners. Let no vandalism or avarice or neglect, no ravages of time testify to the present or to the coming generations that we have forgotten as a people the cost of a free and undivided republic.

If other eyes grow dull, other hands slack, and other hearts cold in the solemn trust, ours shall keep it well as long as the light and warmth of life remain to us.

Let us, then, at the time appointed gather around their sacred remains and garland the passionless mounds above them with the choicest flowers of spring-time; let us raise above them the dear old flag they saved from dishonor; let us in this solemn presence renew our pledges to aid and assist those whom they have left among us—a sacred charge upon a nation's gratitude—the soldiers' and sailors' widow and orphan.

It is the purpose of the Commander-in-Chief to inaugurate this observance with the hope that it will be kept up from year to year, while a survivor of the war remains to honor the memory of his departed comrades. He earnestly desires the public press to lend its friendly aid in bringing it to the notice of comrades in all parts of the country in time for simultaneous compliance therewith.

Department commanders will use every effort to make this order effective.

*By order of
John A. Logan
Commander-in-Chief*

Most Americans still observe Memorial Day but now on a three-day weekend as a convenience. Tragically, this has deteriorated the significance and spirit of the holiday. It has gone from being a day of national mourning and remembrance to a day of parties and barbecues to usher in the summer season.

For many years, the term "Decoration Day" was used by the press and general public to describe May 30. The Grand Army of the Republic, as an organization, never used that term. To them, it was always Memorial Day.

ORCUTT POST NO. 79

The Department of Michigan of the Grand Army of the Republic was first organized in May 6, 1868, by Brevet Brigadier General William Humphrey, former colonel of the 2nd Michigan Infantry, and Brevet Major General Russell A. Alger, former colonel of the 5th Michigan Cavalry. Alger was elected the first Michigan Department commander and, in 1889, commander-in-chief of the Grand Army of the Republic. General Alger would later become a United States senator, governor of Michigan and secretary of war under President William McKinley.

The inaugural effort of forming a chapter of the new veterans' association in Kalamazoo was in 1868, and it was designated as Post No. 5. During the next few years, the national organization of the GAR went through what can be described as growing pains and almost died out. This was due to many veterans thinking that the GAR was just another political organization. Post No. 5 folded in two years, most likely as the state-level organization floundered and simply fell apart. The Department of Michigan ceased to exist in 1872 but was reorganized on January 22, 1879. Though there was not a Grand Army post in Kalamazoo County during those intervening years, Memorial Day was observed by several communities in the county, and the veterans turned out en masse.

In 1882, a new post was organized in Kalamazoo. The veterans who gathered to accomplish this desired to adopt the name Dwight May Post, but the post in Midland, Michigan, had submitted its application for a charter and requested the same name several days before. The Kalamazoo veterans then decided to name the post in honor of their former comrade and Kalamazoo sheriff Benjamin Orcutt. The new post was assigned the number seventy-nine by the department commander. Orcutt Post was officially chartered on September 20, 1882. The fourteen founding members are as follows, including their service and civilian occupations:

Frederick W. Curtenius, Colonel of the 6th Michigan Infantry/Heavy Artillery, president of the Kalamazoo City Bank and elected Kalamazoo Village president in 1866

Dr. Joel A. Partridge, musician, Company F, 112th Ney York Infantry, physician and examining surgeon of pensions

Charles E. Smith, lieutenant colonel, 11th Michigan Cavalry, conveyancer

Amos D. Allen, commissary sergeant, 13th Michigan Infantry, Kalamazoo County clerk and justice of the peace

Deloes Phillips, captain, Company E, 17th Michigan Infantry, owner of the Star Organ Manufacturing Company

Robert P. James, corporal, Company L, 6th Michigan Cavalry and five-time prisoner of war, dentist

John A. Scrivner, Company E, 2nd Nebraska Cavalry, machinist

Robert Hill, first lieutenant, 1st Michigan Sharpshooters, attorney

Stephen H. Wattles, Colonel, 14th Indiana Infantry, builder, village marshal, assistant prosecuting attorney and later a judge

Patrick H. Burke, corporal, Company E, 157th New York Infantry, hotel keeper

Henry J. Ogden, Company I, 9th Michigan Cavalry, postal letter carrier

George M. Buck, sergeant, Company C, 20th Michigan Infantry, attorney and later judge of the ninth district court

Theodore A. Palmer, musician, Company K, 17th Michigan Infantry, grocer

William Tink, corporal, Company E, 13th Michigan Infantry, machine hand at Page Lumber Manufacturing Company

Eight months later, in May 1883, there were ninety-two members of the post. They had tripled their membership. By April 11, 1884, the *Kalamazoo Gazette* reported that Orcutt Post had 150 names on the rolls.

As previously stated, the Grand Army was intended as being a nonpolitical entity. The post in Kalamazoo publicly defended that position in August 1884. The local Republican campaign committee that was supporting General John A. Logan for president of the United States placed a sign on its building that included the membership badge of the GAR. Several members of Post No. 79 demanded that it be removed. They were curtly informed that it would remain until after the election. An emergency meeting of the post was called, and a resolution was adopted condemning the use of the GAR insignia for any political purpose. Members of the post caused such uproar that the "proper authorities" were solicited to remove the insignia from the sign. After pressing the issue, the sign was painted over. The fact

The Postwar Years

Orcutt Post No. 79 Memorial Hall, 115 North Park Street, circa 1920. *Kalamazoo Valley Museum Collection.*

that proper authorities included the sheriff and prosecuting attorney, who were members of Orcutt Post, likely had something to do with the successful end to the matter.

During its lifetime, Post No. 79 had upward of 100 members at any given time, until death finally took its toll. A total of 430 names appear on the roster from chartering to disbandment. The post met on Monday evenings in various places around Kalamazoo, including the Kalamazoo Light Guard Armory, which was located on the second floor of the present Peninsula

Building on the corner of Portage and Michigan Avenue. They also met at the Turn Verein Hall (in the same building as the armory) and the Odd Fellows Hall. Post 79 built a permanent meeting hall at 115 North Park Street, which was dedicated on April 9, 1908.

It was a two-story brick building, with a stained-glass window to the left of the front door. There was a kitchen and dining room on the first floor and the meeting hall on the second floor. In the hallway was a drinking fountain, which was plumbed so that the water would come out of the spout of an upright canteen. It was a play on the motto "we drank from the same canteen," a common adage in the ranks of the GAR, referencing the times when, as soldiers, the men shared their rations and water.

The veterans were involved in several different activities. Entertainment including recitation of poetry, soloists and short plays, most with a patriotic theme, were presented to the public. Bean soup suppers were put on to raise funds. Hundreds of dollars were expended for relief of disabled veterans and the widows and orphans of Kalamazoo and the surrounding area. The minute books of the post have weekly entries of which families were given

Another view of the memorial hall, circa 1908. *Courtesy of Michael Culp.*

food and coal or wood for heat. Those veterans who were ill and could not support their families were recipients of aid. Former soldiers attempting to secure employment were assisted by the post and those members who were prominent in the community.

Another example of the activities of the post was relief for the victims of the Charleston, South Carolina earthquake in 1886. Posts in the Department of Michigan all contributed to the cause. Post 79 raised a total of $151.85. It was the largest contribution of any post in Michigan. Kalamazoo's veterans also raised funds for the victims of the San Francisco earthquake in 1903.

Memorial Day in Kalamazoo was a large event, with hundreds turning out for the ceremony at Riverside. The parade stepped off in the afternoon from the hall on Park Street. Participating were the members of Orcutt Post, the Woman's Relief Corps, Sons of Veterans and the Daughters of Veterans. The Orcutt Post Fife and Drum Corps led the parade, followed by the Post No. 79 United States flag and then the veterans. The Kalamazoo Silver Cornet Band also provided music. Other participating organizations were the Knights Templar, Masons and the fire department. The procession stopped at the bridge over the Kalamazoo River and flowers were scattered into the water in memory of the sailors. The parade then continued up to the GAR lot in Riverside, where the crowds had gathered to witness the ceremonies and listen to the oration of the day, honoring those who had given the "last full measure" to the nation.

Like most posts of the Grand Army of the Republic, Orcutt Post was integrated. On the membership rolls are the names of eight Black veterans: Napoleon Hamilton, Thomas Woodford, James H. Bass, Nathan Beauregard, Samuel Henderson, Rueben Robbins, Simeon Robbins and William H. Roberts. Most of these men served in the 1st Michigan Colored Infantry, designated the 102nd United States Colored Infantry. Napoleon Hamilton was a veteran of the 54th Massachusetts. Reuben Robbins served in the 55th Massachusetts, the sister regiment of the 54th. Several of these men are buried at the GAR lot with their White comrades; there was no segregation, even in death.

Orcutt Corps No. 110, Woman's Relief Corps

In the years following the establishment of the Grand Army, the wives, sisters and mothers of veterans began to organize into ladies' aid societies, with the goal of assisting the veterans in their charitable works. This movement was most prevalent in the New England states. The women would hold fundraising events to raise money to sustain the relief given to the widows and orphans of soldiers and assist disabled veterans. The work performed by these ladies harkened back to the days of the war, as many of these same women worked in the Ladies' Soldiers Aid Societies.

In 1883, at the invitation of the commander-in-chief of the GAR, Paul VanderVort, these women's groups sent representatives to the National Encampment of the Grand Army, with the purpose of uniting all of the societies into one organization. That organization became the National Woman's Relief Corps, Auxiliary to the Grand Army of the Republic.

The Woman's Relief Corps, or WRC, was organized in Michigan on April 2, 1884. Three years later, the women of Kalamazoo decided to organize a corps. On May 3, 1887, the Orcutt Corps No. 110 was chartered by the Department of Michigan, WRC, with twenty-seven members. The charter members were Matilda Keyser, Henrietta Doan, Mary E. Bishop, Helen DeKraker, Anna Robbins, Emily Orcutt, Anna Barnea, Mary Dunbar, Alice Drake, Emma Gifford, Maria Rose, Maria Doubleday, Sarah Harris, Anna Hurd, Sophronia Winters, Elizabeth Keyser, Anna Buck, Jane Partridge, Clara Perkins, Mary E. Burns, Marian Hodges, Lucy M. Scott, Anna Buck, Elizabeth "Bessie" Baird, Agnes d'Arcambal, Emma Peck and Martha Nichols. Emily Orcutt, widow of the late Sheriff Benjamin Orcutt, was elected its first president.

The day after it was chartered, when announcing the formation of the ladies' association, the *Kalamazoo Daily Telegraph* explained the mission of Orcutt Corps: "It is the purpose of the W.R.C. to aid the G.A.R. in charitable and benevolent work for the post and for ex-soldiers and their families outside the G.A.R. Wherever a soldier or his family need encouragement, sympathy and help, there the W.R.C. will be found, a helper and true friend. In many ways they will aid the cause. It promises to be a large and important co-operative society."

Every year, the Woman's Relief Corps put out a call for citizens to donate fresh flowers for the Memorial Day services. Many would drop off the flowers at the GAR hall, and the ladies would tie them into small bouquets to be placed on the graves of deceased soldiers. The comrades would gather at the GAR hall in the morning and divide into two groups—one for Riverside and the other for Mountain Home—and then proceed to the cemeteries and decorate the graves with the flowers prepared by the Relief Corps.

The Postwar Years

Monument on the Orcutt Corps No. 110, Woman's Relief Corps, burial lot, Riverside Cemetery. *Photo by the author.*

Over the years, Orcutt Corps No. 110 expanded its mission. During World War I, it worked alongside the American Red Cross, knitting socks, making soldiers' sewing kits and supplying towels, handkerchiefs and pajamas to the hospital at Fort Custer in Augusta. After the Civil War veterans were gone, the WRC turned its focus to the support of veterans of all wars and their families. Orcutt Corps surrendered its charter in 1986, after ninety-nine years of service to Kalamazoo County. The Woman's Relief Corps still exists in Michigan, continuing its work at the Veterans' Administration Hospital in Augusta and at the Michigan Veterans' Facility in Grand Rapids.

Five other Grand Army of the Republic posts were organized in Kalamazoo County during a time of exponential growth. Unfortunately, the records of these posts have not been located and are feared lost or destroyed. The information contained herein is from several sources.

Joseph Smith Post No. 215

Joseph Smith Post No. 215 of Fulton was chartered on January 12, 1884. To date, there has been no information found about the exact Joseph Smith for whom the post was named. It could be for Joseph L. Smith, who enlisted at Kalamazoo in the 13th Michigan Infantry.

A total of twenty-six members of Post No. 215 have been verified thus far. The post was the next to last of Kalamazoo to surrender its charter in 1930. There were only two veterans known to still be living in Fulton, and presumably, it was too much for them to continue operation of the post.

A monument was erected in the South Fulton Cemetery by the comrades of Post No. 215. It is undated and no information on when it was placed has been located. The monument is unique, as it also acknowledges the role of women in the war effort. The inscriptions on three sides read:

In memory of those who fought for the
preservation of the Union
1861–1865

They fought for their country
For our country they bled
We honor the living
We mourn for the dead

Erected by Joseph Smith Post No. 215
In memory of all loyal women of the war
1861–1865

Acker Post No. 220

Acker Post No. 220 of Vicksburg was chartered on January 13, 1885, and named for George S. Acker of Kalamazoo. Acker enlisted on August 21, 1861, as captain of Company I, 1st Michigan Cavalry. By November 30, 1863, he had been promoted through the ranks to colonel, taking command of the 9th Michigan Cavalry. He was brevetted a brigadier general on March 16, 1865, for "gallant and soldierly conduct under all circumstances…and conspicuous gallantry" in action at Cynthia, Kentucky, in June 1864. He was discharged for disability on June 27, 1865, and died at Kalamazoo,

The Postwar Years

Joseph Smith Post No. 215 monument, South Fulton Cemetery, Fulton. *Photo by the author.*

Michigan, on September 6, 1879. General Acker is buried in Union City, Michigan. When Acker Post surrendered its charter in 1913, several of the comrades transferred their membership to Kalamazoo.

The Acker Corps No. 176, the auxiliary to Acker Post No. 220, erected a red granite monument in 1893, which is located at the entrance of the Schoolcraft Township Cemetery on W Avenue East. The east side is emblazoned with the dedication:

> *Honor To*
> *The Defenders of the Union*
> *Heroes of*
> *1861–1865*
> *Acker Post No. 220*

Acker Post No. 220 monument, Schoolcraft Township Cemetery, Vicksburg. *Photo by the author.*

The west side attributes the monument to the ladies of the auxiliary, the Woman's Relief Corps:

Erected by
W.R.C. No. 176
1893

The Postwar Years

Eugene H. Bronson Post No. 295

Eugene H. Bronson Post No. 295 of Galesburg was chartered on February 7, 1885, and was named for Sergeant Eugene H. Bronson of Comstock. Bronson enlisted in Company C, 4th Michigan Cavalry on August 9, 1862. He was twenty-six years old. Sergeant Bronson died of disease at Nashville, Tennessee, on November 27, 1863, and is buried at Nashville National Cemetery. Very little is known about this post, and only eleven veterans have been verified as having been members. According to newspaper accounts, the post had upward of one hundred members over the years. The post survived for twenty-eight years. There was no known meeting hall built, and it is likely that the post met in the local Masonic or Odd Fellows Hall. Post No. 295 surrendered its charter in 1913. There is no monument or marker in Galesburg honoring the veterans of the Civil War.

Walter Orr Post No. 312

Walter Orr Post No. 312 of Scotts was chartered on June 27, 1885. The name of this post was originally the Lillie Post No. 312, named for Julius Lillie. Lillie was a resident of Pavilion Township and enlisted in Company E, 13th Michigan Infantry as a corporal on September 16, 1861, at the age of twenty-eight. Lillie served through the war, rising to the rank of first lieutenant on March 19, 1864. On March 9, 1865, Lillie was taken prisoner by the rebels. He was exchanged and mustered out of service on July 28, 1865. Grand Army of the Republic regulations directed that a post could be named for a deceased solder or sailor, the name of the city or village in which the post was located or a battle of the war. It could not be verified that Lillie was actually deceased, so caution being the better part of valor, the members decided to change the name to honor Walter Orr.

Walter T. Orr of Climax enlisted in Comapny A, 13th Michigan Infantry, on October 16, 1861. He was wounded in the Battle of Chickamauga, Georgia, on September 19, 1863. Walter lay on the battlefield for four days, until he was taken to the field hospital. He died of his wounds on September 24, 1863, and is buried at the Chattanooga National Cemetery in Tennessee.

On Post No. 312's rolls are the names of 136 veterans. The post met in a building named Union Hall. The charter was surrendered in 1913, and several members transferred to Orcutt Post No. 79.

In 2013, a citizen ad hoc committee, the Friends of the Union Veterans and the 13th Michigan Memorial Association, jointly erected a boulder with a cast bronze plaque on the site of the post meeting hall, now a vacant lot, next to the Scotts Community Center. The plaque reads:

> *On This Site*
> *Stood*
> *Walter Orr Post 312*
> *Grand Army of the Republic*
> *1885–1913*
> *G.A.R.*
> *In Memory of the Boys in Blue*
> *Who Answered Lincoln's Call*
> *To Preserve the Union.*
> *(1861–1865)*
> *Erected 2013 by*
> *Friends of the Union Veterans*
> *&*
> *13th Michigan*
> *Memorial Association*

Burson Post No. 303

Burson Post No. 303 of Schoolcraft was chartered on April 16, 1885. There were five Burson brothers who served in the war. Three survived and when Post 303 was organized, it named the post in honor of the two brothers who sacrificed for the Union. The surviving brothers were Milton, Company L, 5th Michigan Cavalry; Albert, Company F, 3rd Michigan Cavalry; Warren, Company F, 3rd Michigan Cavalry.

Abner H. Burson, corporal, Company L, 5th Michigan Cavalry, died at Schoolcraft on February 24, 1865, of disease contracted during the war. Joseph Burson, Company L, 5th Michigan Cavalry, was killed in action at Hawes Shop, Virginia, on May 28, 1864.

The charter of Burson Post No. 303 was surrendered in 1924. Burson Post erected a memorial dated 1899 in the Schoolcraft Cemetery. An account in the *Kalamazoo Telegraph* from May 1900 announced the dedication. The monument, a black granite obelisk, is cut with the words:

The Postwar Years

Above: Walter Orr Post No. 312 monument, which sits on the site of the memorial hall, Scotts. *Photo by the author.*

Left: Burson Post No. 303 monument, Schoolcraft Cemetery. *Photo by the author.*

1899
In Memory of the
Defenders of our Country
Erected by
Burson Post No. 303
G.A.R.

Although not in Kalamazoo County, the G.L. Hudson Post No. 317, located in Mattawan, Van Buren County, also had several members who lived in Kalamazoo County's Texas Township. Post No. 317 was chartered on August 17, 1885.

THE LAST MAN

The last Civil War veteran of Kalamazoo County, and the last member of Orcutt Post, was Smith H. Carlton.

Carlton enlisted as a private in Company K, 28th Michigan Infantry, at the age of eighteen on February 16, 1865. He was promoted to corporal on November 1, 1865, and was discharged on February 19, 1866, at Raleigh, North Carolina. Smith was part of Sherman's Army that made its famous March to the Sea, from Atlanta to Savannah and then up through the Carolinas. The soldiers were known as Sherman's Bummers.

Smith served as commander of the Department of Michigan, Grand Army of the Republic, from June 1937 to June 1938. In 1938, when it was decided that the GAR hall should be razed to make room for the new federal courthouse and post office, which currently occupies the corner of Michigan Avenue and Park Street, Smith was heartbroken. The morning the wrecking ball arrived to begin its unpleasant task, there sat Smith Carlton on the steps of the building, wearing his Grand Army uniform. He wasn't going anywhere. All he would say was, "I'm protecting my comrades."

A few hours later, and after an abundance of patience on the part of the demolition crew and encouragement from his family, Smith gave up his position and went home. The hall came down. The Joseph Westnedge American Legion Post No. 36 was, at that time, meeting in one of the old homes on South Street, and the members readily agreed to provide a room for the last remaining veterans to meet.

Carlton also served several terms as the commander of Orcutt Post No. 79. In the last few years, he was elected commander by default, as Lewis Sergeant,

The Postwar Years

Left: Smith H. Carlton in his GAR uniform. *Kalamazoo Valley Museum Collection*.

Below: Bronze plaque on the grave of Smith H. Carlton, "The Last Man of Orcutt Post No. 79." Placed by the Sons of Union Veterans of the Civil War. *Photo by the author*.

the next to last surviving veteran, died in January 1940. As the last man of almost two thousand Kalamazoo County residents who were veterans of the Civil War, all he had left was the empty meeting room and the memories of his friends. The loneliness he must have felt would have been dismal.

Smith Carlton died on November 29, 1943, at the age of ninety-six. He was out for his usual early morning constitutional when he was struck by a car while crossing the street. It was a foggy morning, and the driver did not see Smith step off the curb. Smith Carlton's funeral was one of the largest memorial events that Kalamazoo had seen in several years. He is buried at Maple Grove Cemetery on Sprinkle Road near Interstate 94 in the family plot. Besides a granite headstone, a bronze plaque rests on his grave, indicating that he was "The Last Man of Orcutt Post No. 79." It was placed by the John P. Riley Camp No. 12, Sons of Union Veterans of the Civil War.

Orcutt Post ceased to exist, and its charter presumably returned to department headquarters at Lansing. Kalamazoo County's only living link to the Civil War was gone.

The Monuments of Kalamazoo

Monuments and memorials to the Civil War veterans in the city of Kalamazoo include the GAR Tree, located in Bronson Park. The original tree, an elm, was planted in April 1909, on the east side of the park. It soon died and was replaced about a year later with a maple. That tree survived for over one hundred years, until it died of disease. It had even survived the tornado of 1980. The current tree was purchased and planted by the members of the General Benjamin Pritchard Camp No. 20, Sons of Union Veterans of the Civil War, in 2014.

The cannon, a ten-inch Columbiad, was brought to Kalamazoo by Post No. 79 in 1898. It was placed on the northeast corner of the grounds of the Kalamazoo County Courthouse. When the current courthouse was constructed in 1936, the cannon was moved to Patriot Park on top of the hill on Blakeslee Street. The original plan was to eventually move all veterans' memorials to that park, but before it could be accomplished, the State of Michigan built the tuberculosis sanatorium there, and the plan was shelved. In the 1980s, an ad hoc citizens committee was formed, and the cannon was restored and moved to the southeast corner of Bronson Park.

The Postwar Years

Right: New Orcutt Post No. 79 GAR tree, Bronson Park. *Photo by the author.*

Below: Ten-inch Columbiad cannon, Bronson Park. Brought to Kalamazoo by Orcutt Post No. 79 in 1898. *Photo by the author.*

The survivors of the 11th Michigan Cavalry placed a boulder with a bronze plaque in Bronson Park.

> *1863–1913*
> *Presented to the City of*
> *Kalamazoo*
> *This the 11th Day of September, 1913*
> *By the 11th Regiment*
> *Michigan Volunteer Cavalry*
> *On the 50th Anniversary*
> *Of Leaving for the Front*

The only problem is that the adjutant general's records for the state of Michigan maintains that the 11th Cavalry left Kalamazoo for the front on December 17, 1863.

A boulder with an aluminum plaque sits on the island on Egleston Avenue, two blocks east of Portage Street. The original bronze plaque was stolen

The 11th Michigan Cavalry monument, Bronson Park. *Photo by the author.*

and, in the early 1980s, was replaced with another cast plaque. This was stolen within six months of replacement. The aluminum plaque was placed in 2005 by the Sons of Union Veterans of the Civil War. The text reads:

> *This stone, placed here October, 1923, by the surviving members of the Twenty-fifth Michigan Volunteer Infantry who served in the Civil War, marks the spot where this regiment first went into camp, September 1, 1862, was mustered into the service of the United States, September 22, 1862, and left for the front, October 1, 1862, under its gallant and beloved commanders, Colonel Orlando H. Moore, Lieut. Col. Benj. F. Orcutt. This regiment participated in 22 battles, was mustered out at Salisbury, North Carolina, June 24, 1865, and was discharged from the service at Jackson, Mich. , July 14, 1865, after having gallantly performed its part toward the preservation of the union and won for itself a merited reputation for bravery and loyalty.*

Of great concern to the comrades of Orcutt Post was the fact that, early on, several former soldiers were being buried in unmarked graves at potter's field on the north end of Riverside Cemetery. Through the efforts of General William Shakespeare, the post was given a burial lot located on Section H in Riverside Cemetery. The lot was presented to the post by the City of Kalamazoo and was formally dedicated on May 30, 1888. Kalamazoo mayor Otto Ihling made the official presentation, and Comrade William Shakespeare responded for the post. Soon after, the remains of five veterans who had been buried at potter's field and elsewhere in the cemetery were exhumed and reburied at the new soldiers' lot.

The part of the lot across the road in Section R was given to the post in 1899. Burials began on that side in 1902. There was a wooden flagpole placed on Section R about this same time. It was replaced with the current flagpole on Section H on May 26, 1916, which was donated by Bond Supply Company and erected by Consumers' Power Company.

The memorial on Section H was erected in two phases. The first was the base and shaft of rough gray granite. That part was placed in 1899. It was the post's intention to have a bronze statue of a Union Civil War soldier placed on top, but it could not raise enough money to pay for bronze, so a cheaper statue of made of granite was purchased. The memorial was dedicated on September 22, 1901. Three thousand people were in attendance. The comrades of Orcutt Post raised the money themselves, with the help of the Woman's Relief Corps. There were no public funds expended for this memorial.

Left: The 25th Michigan Infantry monument, Egleston Avenue, circa 1925. *Kalamazoo Valley Museum Collection.*

Below: Modern view of 25th Michigan Infantry monument. *Photo by the author.*

Above: Orcutt Post No. 79 burial lot, Section H, Riverside Cemetery. *Photo by the author.*

Left: Soldiers' Memorial, Section H, Riverside Cemetery, circa 1940s. *Kalamazoo Valley Museum Collection.*

At the GAR lot are buried 125 veterans. Several of those interred at the lot were residents of the Michigan Soldiers' Home in Grand Rapids and were transferred to the Kalamazoo Asylum for the Insane, where they died. It can be said that several of these men likely suffered from what we now refer to as post-traumatic stress disorder. In the late nineteenth century, it was referred to as "soldiers' heart" and thought to be related to physical heart problems. As doctors didn't know what it actually was and had no way to treat it, the only option was to admit them to the asylum. General Shakespeare also made arrangements with the asylum so that when a veteran died, the GAR would be notified if there was no one to claim the remains. In these cases, General Shakespeare would have the body taken to Herrington's Funeral Parlor, and Post No. 79 would pay the expenses. In later years, Kalamazoo County set aside funds for the burial expenses of indigent veterans. The sum of fifty-five dollars was expended. This included the coffin, a robe to bury the veteran in, the undertaker's fee, digging the grave and transportation of the deceased to the cemetery. A detail from the Orcutt Post would act as pallbearers.

Two granite benches were placed on the burial lot on September 20, 2016. One, placed by the 13th Michigan Memorial Association, is inscribed, "In Memory of the 13th Michigan Infantry, 'Kalamazoo's Own.'" The second, placed by the General Benjamin Pritchard Camp No. 20, Sons of Union Veterans of the Civil War, is engraved, "In Memory of Orcutt Post No. 79, Grand Army of the Republic."

We know some interesting details about those buried at the GAR lot. Two of the veterans died of "cerebral softening," which we now understand to be a symptom of late-stage syphilis. Several were indigent and had no family to care for them or did not have the money to purchase a private cemetery plot. Some of the veterans wished to be buried at the lot simply to be with other veterans. The ties of comradeship were that strong. A few of the veterans' wives were buried at the adjoining Woman's Relief Corps burial lot. Thirteen interred were Black. Over twenty men died in the Michigan Asylum for the Insane on Oakland Drive. One veteran was a police detective with the Kalamazoo Village Police Department. Five were sailors. Four were prisoners of war, and two of those survived Andersonville. One of the other two was only thirteen years old when captured and taken to a camp in Texas. Two veterans committed suicide—one by an overdose of morphine, and the other slit his own throat. One of the Black men was able to pass himself off as White. One died sitting in a bar in downtown Kalamazoo. He was dead for over an hour before it was discovered that he had died. One saved

The Postwar Years

Post No. 79 annex, Section R, Riverside Cemetery. *Photo by the author.*

the life of his childhood friend on the battlefield. The two remained close friends throughout their lives. One was a semiprofessional baseball player. He is buried holding an urn containing the cremated remains of his beloved wife. One was severely wounded on the second day of Gettysburg, when his regiment, the 111th New York Infantry, was pulled out of the defensive line at the Bryan Farm on Cemetery Ridge and sent to help secure the gap in the line and support the 1st Minnesota Infantry when it charged across the field. One was murdered in a bar fight. His right arm had been amputated due to a severe wound received in battle in 1864.

The veterans are gone now. All that is left are a few scattered reminders that they were here. Sometimes we find ourselves thinking of the veterans in the abstract. When we discuss the battles, the hardships, the experiences of the Civil War, we don't usually think of the faces or names of the individual, common soldier. We talk about the generals and their corps, or brigades, the colonels and their regiments and what they did. But the war was on a personal level. It was the neighbor next door, the son or brother or father, the grandfather missing an arm from a wound received at Perryville, Kentucky, or the man on the street walking with a crutch who lost his leg at Gettysburg.

Reunion of the 13th Michigan Infantry at Kalamazoo. Taken in front of the post office, Circa 1913. *Kalamazoo Valley Museum Collection.*

Perhaps on Memorial Day, you will take the time to go to Riverside Cemetery and visit the Orcutt Post lot. Wander around the lot and read the names and regiments on the headstones and remember the words of the Reverend Henry W. Harvey, commander of Orcutt Post in 1917:

> *As for us, we are making our final bow to the world. We know that the world will surge on without us. We only trust that it will never quite forget the old veterans of 1861–1865.*
>
> *Without a lament, with a courage as high as when we were young, we stand upon the firing line. As we fall, it remains a sacred duty to bear each other in turn to the silent resting place.*
>
> *Neath emblems of flowers and a flag and with a final salute, we leave him alone with his glory.*

9
STORIES OF THE VETERANS

Presented here are just a few of the many stories associated with the veterans of Kalamazoo County. Sometimes we forget that the faceless names and dates on a headstone represent a life—a life filled with joy, sorrow and personal challenges. Among the white marble headstones on the Orcutt Post burial lot, there are stories of bravery on the field of battle and, at times, the personal struggle of adjusting to civilian life after the war. For many veterans, the war really never ended.

GEORGE K. SHANNON

In April 1861, Confederate forces fired on Fort Sumter, and the Civil War began. Across the country, in cities and villages, men and boys clamored to sign up to fight. In the village of Kalamazoo in southwest Michigan, it was the same. Two young men, George Shannon, twenty years old, and William Shakespeare, only seventeen, signed up with the 2nd Michigan Infantry. Company K was made up of men primarily from Kalamazoo, and everyone knew one another. George and William were good friends. George was a private, and William, who was good at reading and writing, was appointed corporal and was eventually promoted to sergeant. The 2nd Infantry was assigned to the Army of the Potomac and saw fighting throughout Virginia at places like Blackburn's Ford, both First and Second

Bull Run, White Oak Swamp and Fredericksburg. Later, the 2nd was transferred to the western theater of the war. It was sent to Mississippi and participated in the Siege of Vicksburg.

The 2nd Michigan boys were seasoned soldiers when they found themselves in the Battle of Jackson, Mississippi, on May 14, 1863. The regiment was ordered to advance on the Confederate lines. It was said that "the bullets flew past them like a shower of snowflakes." While the regiment was advancing, both George and William were wounded. They lay on the battlefield for most of the day, no more than ten feet from each other. George had a gunshot wound in his left thigh. William had been shot through both hips, fracturing them. While they lay there, William received several more wounds from stray bullets. In all, he was shot eight times. When the battle ended, members of the 2nd Michigan came back onto the field to pick up the dead and wounded. They found George and began to place him on a stretcher. George raised up his head and protested, saying, "No, don't take me. William is wounded worse than I am, and he should be taken first." William was taken first, and George soon followed him to the field hospital.

Eventually, George was well enough to return to the regiment. William, on the other hand, was so riddled with bullets that the surgeon said there was nothing he could do for him. An account of this appears in the Record of Service of the 2nd Michigan Infantry:

> *Dr. Cleland came back to William with a letter, saying to him that he had written to his mother of his unfortunate condition. Was there any final message to add? William insisted on seeing the letter. Finally, the Doctor read it to him. William said "I want to add a few words to it." "Why", said the doctor, "do you think you can write?" "Yes," said William, "I think I can scrawl out a few words if you prop me up." So the doctors complied with the request, and after propping him up, he added to that letter these words: "Do not be alarmed, dear mother, the doctor is mistaken. I am going to get well and come back to you." Sometime after that, William was brought up to the general hospital at Cincinnati, where he lay for nine long months on his back, in agony, unable to move from one side to the other, and during all that time the doctors were in doubt about his final recovery. But his obstinate determination not to die and to come back to that dear mother pulled him through to final recovery.*

Meanwhile, George had resumed his duties in the regiment. He was taken prisoner near Knoxville, in East Tennessee, on January 11, 1864, and sent to a prisoner of war camp in Georgia, called Camp Sumter, also known as Andersonville. The conditions at Andersonville were horrific. Built to hold only five thousand prisoners, it held a total of over forty-five thousand for the period of its operation. Almost thirteen thousand Union soldiers died there from disease and starvation.

During George's stay in Andersonville, he undoubtedly witnessed the trial and hanging of the leaders of the notorious Raiders, a large group of soldiers who joined together and robbed other soldiers. The Raiders would steal anything from valuables to blankets to food. If resisted, they would beat their victims, sometimes to death. Another group of soldiers banded together to stop the violence, called the Regulators. The six leaders of the Raiders were soon caught and, with the permission of Confederate authorities, were put on trial, found guilty and, on July 11, 1864, hanged for their crimes. These men were buried face down and separate from the other prisoners' graves. This event must have left a lasting impression on young George.

He was taken from there to Venus Point, Georgia, where he was released on November 20 of the same year. George mustered out of the 2nd Michigan on February 20, 1865, at Detroit. After returning to Kalamazoo, George worked as a hack driver, what we would call today a cab driver, although horse drawn. He worked for thirty-plus years and made about eight dollars per week. It was said that he attended more weddings and births than anyone in Kalamazoo, since he was most often the one to take the bride or groom to the minister and was the favorite of all of the doctors in Kalamazoo.

George contracted pneumonia and died on January 10, 1906, and was buried at the soldiers' lot. An account of his funeral was published in the *Kalamazoo Evening Telegraph* on Wednesday, January 10, 1906:

> FLAG WRAPPED
> *Body of George Shannon is Laid to Rest*
> *With the stars and stripes wrapped around the casket and a number of old soldiers with bare heads standing at the grave, the body of George Shannon was placed in the soldier's field at Riverside cemetery this morning. The funeral services were held at 10 o'clock this morning at Herrington's funeral chapel in North Rose Street and were largely attended by Civil War veterans. The services were simple but impressive. The Rev. Caroline Bartlett Crane officiated. Those acting as pall bearers were Horace and James Fuller, George Downey, George Clark, Enoch Shaffer and Charles Hogle.*

Left: Grave of George Shannon, GAR lot, Riverside Cemetery. *Photo by the author.*

Below: Grave of General William Shakespeare, Section L, Riverside Cemetery. *Photo by the author.*

Stories of the Veterans

William Shakespeare did finally return to Kalamazoo after the war. He studied law and became a successful attorney and a prominent citizen. William married and had several children, one of whom founded the Shakespeare Rod and Reel Company. William was also appointed adjutant general of the state militia, with the rank of brigadier general. He was elected commander of the Department of Michigan, Grand Army of the Republic, in 1896. When George Shannon joined the Orcutt Post No. 79, it was William who proudly pinned George's membership badge on him. For all those years after the war, George and William remained the best of friends. When he learned of George's death, William said that it was George's selflessness that saved his life. William died in 1907 from complications from his wounds. He is buried on an adjacent hill overlooking the soldier's lot in Riverside Cemetery.

JOHN BIGHAM

In the original records of Riverside Cemetery of burials on Section H, there is an entry in the records of only the last name "Bigham" and the burial date of April 30, 1894.

An article in the *Kalamazoo Gazette*, dated August 16, 1890, states, "United States Marshal Clarke returned late last night from Kalamazoo and brought with him an old man named Bigham, who is wanted by the government on a charge of impersonating his brother to obtain a pension." It continues:

> *He had no relatives, his only brother, William Bigham, having died about five years ago. He was a veteran of the Civil War, and about a year ago, the old man got hold of his brother's papers. He went before a pension examiner, announced his name as William Bigham, presented his brother's papers and secured the pension. He then applied for admission in the Soldiers' Home, showed the papers and was admitted under the name of his brother. For about a year he lived at his ease at the expense of the state and received a pension. A few days ago, however, the pension department discovered that William Bigham was dead, and began to make inquiries. The old man got wind of the brewing trouble and fled. He was arrested yesterday afternoon by Marshal Clarke about seven miles south of Kalamazoo. He is so feeble that he had to be carried from the hack into the jail.*

Another *Kalamazoo Gazette* article, dated August 20, 1890, under "News from Comstock," read, "John Bigham who was arrested for using his brother's papers and reputation to obtain a pension, was a member of Co. E, 13th Michigan Volunteer Infantry, and was at the Battle of Pittsburg Landing. He enlisted under Capt. John Webb and Lt.s B.F. Broadwell and A.G. Hopkins of Comstock. It is not known by his friends here that he was ever a pauper."

The State of Michigan's records of the 13th Michigan Infantry stated, "Bingham, John, Kalamazoo County. Enlisted in Company E, Thirteenth Infantry, Sept. 15, 1861, at Kalamazoo, for 3 years, age 41. Mustered Jan. 17, 1862. Accidentally wounded. Discharged Sept. 3, 1862." According to the adjutant general's report, John was five feet, six inches tall, had a light complexion, blue eyes and auburn hair.

Another article from the *Gazette*, titled "Comstock Clatter," in April 1894, read, "John Bigham has been taken to Borgess hospital, where he is hardly expected to recover. His disease is dropsy. He is past 70 years of age." (Dropsy was the common name given to congestive heart failure, due to the accumulation of water in the soft tissue.)

A few days later, the *Gazette* announced, "John Bigham, the old soldier who died at Borgess Hospital Saturday night has been well known in this community for more than forty years. His health has been poor and he has been feeble for a long time. We learn that he was buried by the GAR in their grounds at Riverside Cemetery yesterday."

Grave of John Bigham, GAR lot, Riverside Cemetery. *Photo by the author.*

But the question still stands—why didn't John apply for a pension on his own merits of serving in the 13th Michigan Infantry? Why did he have to impersonate his brother William to get a pension and be admitted to the Soldiers' Home? John's pension record from the National Archives in Washington, D.C., gives the answer. When John was wounded, he went to the hospital. Somehow, he was reported as having deserted, so he was ineligible for a pension or admittance to the Soldiers' Home. In John's pension file is a document showing the desertion charge being dismissed on December 24, 1892, two years after the fraud incident, and an application for pension submitted on John's behalf by Charles Foote, a pension attorney in Kalamazoo, who was also a former corporal in the 3rd New York Cavalry.

The sad end of the story is that the pension was approved on January 3, 1893. John died on April 28, 1894. After all of the trouble, he only collected the pension for sixteen months.

Ellis McGerry

Ellis McGerry was born a slave in Kentucky in 1841. At the outbreak of the Civil War, Ellis escaped the plantation and made his way north to Ohio. In 1863, the 55th Massachusetts Infantry was formed, the sister regiment to the 54th Massachusetts Infantry. Ellis enlisted on May 23, 1863, as a private. He was discharged on August 31, 1865, at Mount Pleasant, South Carolina.

The 55th fought at the Battle of Honey Hill, South Carolina, on November 30, 1864. It fought alongside the 32nd, 35th and 102nd U.S. Colored Infantry and the 54th Massachusetts. It was engaged in other actions, including Deveaux Neck, St. Stephens and several on James Island, all located in South Carolina. Ellis was wounded in one of these actions, although it is not known at this time which one.

Following the war, Ellis came to Kalamazoo. It is quite possible that he came here with other Black veterans. Simeon Robbins, who resided in Kalamazoo and is buried in Section V of Riverside Cemetery, also served in the 55th Massachusetts.

Ellis worked as a day laborer during his life in Kalamazoo. By the time of his death, Ellis was living in a shack in the alley off North Street. It is estimated that Ellis died on January 1, 1907. Ellis was always seen walking about town and was well known in his neighborhood. He had been missed a few days when it was determined that something was wrong. His friend Riley Burton, a veteran of the 67th Indiana Infantry, had not seen Ellis

Grave of Ellis McGerry, GAR lot, Riverside Cemetery. *Photo by the author.*

for some time, so he went to check on him. Riley found the door to the shack bolted from the inside, and hearing no response to his knocking, he broke the door down. There, he found Ellis's lifeless body on his bed. The cause of death was listed as "bladder trouble." Ellis was taken to Truesdale's Funeral Home, and services were held at the Second Baptist Church on Thursday, January 3. Ellis was buried by the GAR at their lot.

Ira H. Curtiss

Many of the veterans buried at the lot had broken down physically, the strain of the war taking its toll on them. For some, the horrors of war affected them emotionally. Some were able to contain it, while others held out for as long as they could, until they reached a breaking point. It was this way with Ira H. Curtiss.

Ira was born in 1849 in Wallingford, Connecticut, the son of Hubbard and Elizabeth Curtiss. Hubbard was a spoon maker by trade. Ira had two sisters, Lilla and Catherine, and a brother, Francis. Ira reenlisted in the U.S. Navy at Brooklyn, New York, on July 27, 1864, and served aboard the USS *Maratanza* as a first-class boy. He was fifteen years old. It is noted in the records of the *Maratanza* that he had previously served on the USS *Minnesota* and the USS *Vermont* at the same rank; however, those records have not been located.

The descriptive roll from the *Maratanza* says that Ira was five feet tall and had gray eyes, light hair and a fair complexion. He was discharged from the navy on July 25, 1867, and lived in Cincinnati for a while. Eventually, he made his way to Allegan, Michigan. There he met Eva Pierce, who he would marry on December 19, 1877. Ira worked as a butcher. It is known from newspaper accounts that Ira and Eva had at least one child. The couple divorced in 1894. Ira moved to Kalamazoo, and Eva and the child went to Oakland, California, where her sister lived. Ira resided at 121 Buckley Street in Kalamazoo, and he is not listed as a member of the GAR.

In 1895, Ira was working at the Michigan Asylum for the Insane as a meat cutter in the kitchen. It is about this time that things came to the breaking point for Ira. On Thursday, September 12, 1895, the *Kalamazoo Gazette* ran the headline "Suddenly Insane: The Asylum Meat Cutter Suicides." The article read:

Stories of the Veterans

A suicide, the details of which were very much out of the usual order occurred at the asylum about 9 o'clock Wednesday morning. Ira H. Curtiss, who for nearly two years has been the meat cutter at the asylum, ended his life by slashing his throat with a large steak knife. He was seen by a patient named John Hobbs, who attempted to thwart Curtiss in his apparent determination to end his life, but Curtiss turned on him, and Hobbs had to defend himself with a cleaver. He managed to escape, and Adam Grant heard the racket and rushed into the meat cutting room. Curtiss also attacked him, and he, too, had to defend himself. Curtiss slashed his own throat with the knife, cutting off the windpipe and several small arteries. He rushed out of the room, knife in hand, and ran as fast as his failing strength would permit, and fell down after going about 35 rods. Mr. Grant was close by him and summoned the doctors and an attempt was made to sew up the injury, but he died before it could be completed.

The article goes on to say that at two o'clock that morning, Ira was out on the grounds and requested the night watchman take him to see one of the doctors. The watchman could see that Ira "wasn't quite right," so he took him to see Dr. Edwards. Ira was delusional, saying that there were "hundreds of men and women trying to kill him." Dr. Edwards was able to calm him and sent him to his room. Dr. Edwards also told the watchman to keep an eye on him.

Grave of Ira H. Curtis, GAR lot, Riverside Cemetery. *Photo by the author.*

Ira was buried at the soldiers' lot in Riverside on Friday, September 13. The very next day, the *Kalamazoo Gazette* reported an interesting development: "A woman whom Ira Curtiss when alive introduced as Mrs. Brown, was on deck at the funeral yesterday as the only mourner. She declared that she was Curtiss' wife, that they were married last August, but had not allowed anyone to know about their secret. She declines to state where or by whom they were married. There seems to be a mystery connected with the affair. The alleged wedding day was not far from the time he secured his back pension allowance. There was $41 due the deceased from the asylum and $40 on pension account from the bank."

In the *Gazette* the following day, another article appeared, saying that Mrs. Curtiss thought foul play was involved in her husband's death. A woman with whom Mrs. Curtiss was boarding made a few comments to the press and other interested parties on behalf of the widow. She said that Mrs. Curtiss did not believe her husband committed suicide but that it was John Hobbs who killed him. She admitted that Ira had been a drinker and that the alcohol had made him unstable. The woman also made the statement that Mrs. Curtiss did not want any of the money belonging to her husband. This is where the story goes cold. In spite of further research, "Mrs. Curtiss" disappeared from Kalamazoo altogether.

Stanley B. Cowing

Stanley Bagge Cowing was born in Buffalo, New York, in 1844, to Harrison and Louise Cowing. He was one of nine children. Stanley enlisted in Company K, 2nd New York Mounted Rifles, on February 22, 1865, and was discharged on August 10, 1865, at Petersburg, Virginia. According to the U.S. Census, Stanley worked for the Warren Roofing Company and resided at 921 Prospect Avenue in Buffalo. He also played baseball for the Niagara Club, a city baseball team in Buffalo. A few years later, Stanley met and married the love of his life, Wilma Peck, who was born in 1860. They were married in 1891, most likely in New York. Stanley and Wilma were living in Chicago in 1900, where he worked putting in cement sidewalks and she worked as a stenographer. Stanley's father, Harrison, died in Buffalo in 1899, and his mother, Louise, died in Kalamazoo in 1911.

The Cowings had no children. Wilma died in Kalamazoo on March 14, 1910. Stanley was devastated. An article in the *Kalamazoo Gazette* told the story:

> *The love between Stanley B. Cowing and his wife was the kind that death could not end—the love that poets delight to sing about, and around which the most beautiful romances in the world have been woven. After a long and happy life together, the wife died nearly ten years ago, and the bereaved husband, abhorring the thought of consigning to the cold earth the body of his loved one, carried out a plan by which this could be avoided.*
>
> *Enlisting the services of G.P. Truesdale, undertaker, Mr. Cowing had the corpse of his wife cremated, and the ashes hermetically sealed*

Stories of the Veterans

Grave of Stanley and Wilma Cowing, GAR lot, Riverside Cemetery. *Photo by the author.*

in a mortuary urn. This he placed in Mr. Truesdale's care, for the idea of consigning it to a cold niche in a mausoleum was almost as repulsive to him as to have it buried under six feet of earth. Thereafter, Mr. Cowing gave to the vase, which held the pitiful remains of all he held dear in life, all the devoted attention of a heartbroken lover. Daily he placed before it, as before a shrine, the loveliest flowers he could procure. His whole life seemed to be spent in thoughts of his lost wife, and in showing, by his daily offerings of flowers, how vividly she still dwelt in his memory. But, his service to his loved one, like all beautiful and perfect things, came to an end. Broken in health, Mr. Cowing was no longer able to earn a living for himself.

Lacking means of support, he applied to the Old Soldiers' Home at Grand Rapids for admission, and went there to live. The precious urn holding the ashes of his wife he per force left behind, in Mr. Truesdale's care.

For many months, Mr. Truesdale heard nothing whatever from Mr. Cowing. What to do with Mrs. Cowing's ashes and their receptacle was a question to which he could find no acceptable answer.

At the Soldiers' Home, Mr. Cowing had felt his death was not far off. An overpowering impulse had taken possession of him, to return to Kalamazoo and visit once more his wife's mortuary urn, holding silent communion with the memories that were his, of their happy life together.

Mr. Truesdale received a notification that his services as undertaker were needed at Borgess Hospital. An old man, a former soldier in the union Army had died there. When Mr. Truesdale saw the one awaiting him, he instantly recognized him as Stanley Cowing, the man who for so long a time had paid a daily visit, bearing flowers to the urn in which his idolized wife's ashes lay.

When Stanley had reached Kalamazoo, he was too seriously ill to carry out his plans. Instead of making the visit to which he had looked forward to so eagerly, he was taken to Borgess, and died there without ever again having an opportunity to pay a loving tribute in flowers to the wife he had loved so well.

Though separated by life, the devoted lovers were united by death. Mr. Truesdale, believing that Stanley's dearest wish would be to have the urn *he had treasured in life constantly with him in death, placed the urn in Stanley's coffin, and together as they had lived, they were buried.*

Stanley passed away at Borgess in Kalamazoo on February 11, 1921. He and Wilma were separated for almost eleven years. To this day, there is no official record of Wilma being buried with Stanley.

BENJAMIN F. STEWART

Sometimes, keeping a little secret can be a bit unnerving. Keeping a big secret can make life difficult, or it just might make it easier. Benjamin Stewart had a big secret.

Benjamin died on January 11, 1918, at the age of seventy-four, at his home at 1419 Third Street in Kalamazoo. For many years, he worked in Kalamazoo as a common laborer, picking up jobs where and when he could. He and his third wife, Jane "Jennie" Powers, had a good home and made a life with each other. There really was nothing remarkable about Benjamin. His death record states that he was a married White male and died of paralysis of the heart.

Before coming to Kalamazoo, Benjamin lived in Cass County, Michigan. He had been married twice before. His first wife, Rachel Todd, died in 1870. He was then married to a sixteen-year-old girl by the name of Grace. Her maiden name is not found, and a record of marriage has yet to be discovered. In 1915, records reveal that he had one living child. It is not known which of Benjamin's wives was the child's mother.

Benjamin was born in Georgia on March 27, 1846, to Rodrick and Lucretia Stewart. By the 1860s, Benjamin was living in Union Township, Mercer County, Ohio. He enlisted in the Union army on September 29, 1864, at Cincinnati, as a private. He served until his discharge on September 30, 1865, at Nashville, Tennessee, where he mustered out with his regiment. He suffered a bayonet wound in the left thigh at the Battle of Nashville.

Grave of Benjamin F. Stewart, GAR lot, Riverside Cemetery. *Photo by the author.*

Benjamin did not join the Grand Army of the Republic. It is doubtful that he attended any soldier reunions at all. If he had, his secret would have been revealed. His secret was that he was Black, and he and Jennie were passing as White.

Benjamin enlisted in the Union army in Company K, 15th United States Colored Infantry. The 1880 census lists him and his wife, Grace, as "mulatto." The *Records of Indigent Burials for the County of Kalamazoo* lists Benjamin as White, serving in the 15th United States Infantry. There is no mention of the regiment being the 15th United States Colored Infantry. This and his death certificate made identification of his military service very difficult, even in the twenty-first century. Jennie died in 1924 and is buried at the Woman's Relief Corps lot, adjacent to the Post No. 79 lot in Riverside. This secret that they both took to the grave likely made Benjamin and Jennie's lives a lot easier in the late nineteenth and early twentieth centuries.

Henry O. Barker

Henry Oscar Barker was born in England in either 1845 or 1850, depending on which record you look at. His father's name was listed as Henry, but his mother's name is not mentioned in any records that were found. The Barker family came to the United States and resided in Ottawa, Illinois.

On October 18, 1863, he enlisted in the U.S. Navy at the age of thirteen. For one year, he served as a first-class boy aboard the USS *Queen City*. The descriptive book of the ship described Henry as four feet, nine inches tall, with blue eyes, light hair and a "ruddy complexion." He could not read or write. Descriptive books in the military served a unique purpose. They existed so that if an enlistee deserted, there was a record of the individual that could be used to hunt them down.

The USS *Queen City* is described as having a complement of sixty-five sailors and nine guns. Its assignment was to keep the portion of the White River near Duvall's Bluff clear and free from rebel control. On June 24, 1864, the ship was attacked by Colonel Joseph Shelby's Confederate cavalry on the White River, near the town of Clarendon, Arkansas. During the fight, Henry was wounded by an exploding shell that singed his eyes. The *Queen City* was seized, the crew taken prisoner and the ship burned. Henry and most of the crew were sent to Texas and spent time in a prisoner of war camp. The sailors were first taken to Cotton Plant, Arkansas, and later moved to

Grave of Henry O. Barker, GAR lot, Riverside Cemetery. *Photo by the author.*

Turks Island. Henry was paroled in the fall of 1864 at Duvall's Bluff, Arkansas. He was discharged from service on November 17, 1865, at Mound City, Illinois. He later reenlisted in the navy and was honorably discharged in 1867.

After the war, he was a painter. On July 25, 1888, Henry married Melvina E. Locke at Lacon, Illinois. Sadly, Melvina committed suicide at Westmorland, Pennsylvania, on November 2, 1889. She was buried at Sugar Plain Cemetery in Thorntown, Indiana. Henry and Melvina had no children.

As the years went by, Henry eventually went blind, a result of the exploding shell during the fight with the Confederate cavalry. He was admitted to the Michigan Soldiers' Home with blindness and kidney trouble on July 23, 1891, and on May 19, 1894, was admitted to the Kalamazoo Asylum for the Insane.

Henry's records of death are interesting. Yes, *records* of death. The Kalamazoo County Clerk's records say that Henry died in the asylum on September 17, 1895, at the age of forty-five, of general paresis. The Kent County Clerk's office reports Henry O. Barker died of Paresis on September 17, 1895, in Grand Rapids Township at forty-seven years old and that his occupation was a carriage maker. The *Kalamazoo Gazette* states that Henry "died at the Asylum Tuesday of paresis. He had been an inmate of the institute for 18 months." It is only speculation, but it is possible that his death was reported to the Soldiers' Home by the asylum, as Henry was transferred from that facility, and someone reported it to the Kent County Clerk, who mistakenly recorded the death in the city ledger.

Edward S. Taylor

Edward Taylor was born in Penfield, Calhoun County, Michigan, near Battle Creek, in 1839. At the age of twenty-three, he traveled to Dearborn, where he enlisted as a bugler in Company A, 1st Michigan Sharpshooters, on March 20, 1863. He was mustered into federal service on April 13, 1863, and was married to Miss Mary Wagner on May 2, 1863.

The 1st Sharpshooters took part in many major battles in the western theater of the war. It fought at the Wilderness, Spottsylvania, North Anna, Cold Harbor, the Crater and Hatcher's Run, to name a few. The Michigan Sharpshooters were also part of the Siege of Petersburg, Virginia. When the city fell, the mayor surrendered to Colonel Ralph Ely, who commanded the 8th Michigan Infantry. The Sharpshooters was the first Union regiment to enter the city and raised its regimental colors over the courthouse. A few minutes later, the colors of the 2nd Michigan Infantry, of which many Kalamazoo boys were part, floated over the customs house.

Edward was mustered out with his regiment on July 28, 1865, at Delaney House in Washington, D.C., after participating in the Grand Review of the Union Armies. He returned to Michigan and lived a quiet life and began to collect a pension for disability in June 1889. He was admitted to the asylum at Kalamazoo in late 1891 or early 1892, as he was still listed in the 1890 census as residing in Battle Creek at that time. Edward died on March 21, 1892, in the asylum. The cause of death was erysipelas, which is a bacterial infection that causes large red patches on the skin, especially on the face and legs.

This might have been the end of Edward's story, except for the fact that there was no family to claim the body, and it was decided by the officials at the asylum to send Edward's remains to the medical school of the University of Michigan at Ann Arbor. The commander of Farragut Post No. 32, GAR, of Battle Creek was notified of Edward's passing and sent a telegram to General William Shakespeare in Kalamazoo. General Shakespeare immediately went to the asylum, claimed the body and made arrangements to have Edward interred at Riverside Cemetery in the soldiers' lot. The next afternoon, at 5:00 p.m., Edward was buried with honors by members of the Grand Army of the Republic.

Grave of Edward S. Taylor, GAR lot, Riverside Cemetery. *Photo by the author.*

Arthur d'Armand

Arthur d'Armand was born in France in 1827. He married Miss Marie Porter in Coldwater, Branch County, Michigan, on Christmas Eve, 1879. He is buried at the GAR lot with a headstone that says he served in Company D, 12th New York Cavalry. By 1876, Arthur was living in Kalamazoo and had become a professor of foreign languages at Kalamazoo College. In his off-hours from the college, he gave private French lessons. The April 26, 1876 *Kalamazoo Gazette* reported on the "French Entertainment" held at Dr. Mottram's. The parlors were filled to capacity by the public, where they enjoyed piano, singing and recitation by Arthur's students. The *Gazette* continued, saying, "It was a pleasant evening for everyone, and Prof. d'Armand deserves high credit for his enthusiastic perseverance with his French pupils." Between 1876 and 1887, there appears several news items in both the *Kalamazoo Gazette* and the *Kalamazoo Telegraph* referring to Arthur and praising him for his work and popularity in the community.

Eventually, and for some unknown reason, Arthur left Kalamazoo and moved to Allegan, Michigan, becoming a typewriter salesman. The *Kalamazoo Gazette* reported in April 1885, "Professor d'Armand, a former well-known French master in this city, was sent to the asylum in this city from Allegan Wednesday. The professor's many friends in this city will wish him a speedy recovery from his disturbing illness."

Just a year or so later, the *Kalamazoo Gazette* ran an article titled "Prof. d'Armand Dying: End of a very eventful and romantic career—a brief outline of his life." The article says that as a young man, Arthur came to the United States, landing in New Orleans, and began a career as a salesman for Singer Sewing Machines. The article continues, "Then the war broke out and he was impressed into the confederate service, and was accused of being a spy. In vain he produced the most complete documentary evidence that he was not subject to impressments or draft." It also says that he was able to escape the

Grave of Arthur d'Armand, GAR lot, Riverside Cemetery. *Photo by the author.*

Confederate army and join with a Union regiment, fighting gallantly until he was discharged from the Union army.

Arthur died in the asylum on January 10, 1887. He was originally buried at Section M of Riverside Cemetery but was exhumed and moved to the GAR lot, along with the white marble headstone from the government that was placed shortly after his death. After extensive research, no record can be found to prove that he ever joined the 12th New York Cavalry or any Union regiment. Perhaps the paperwork was lost. Perhaps he never joined the Union army. Perhaps he was never forced to join the Confederate army. Perhaps he wasn't even French.

Cyrus S. Welch

Cyrus S. Welch was born in Stratsbourogh, Portage County, Ohio, in 1839, the son of William and Nancy Welch. He came to Michigan before 1860, settling in Gaines Township, Kent County, and took up farming. On October 25, 1861, Cyrus enlisted as a private for three years in Company G, 13th Michigan Infantry, at Allegan. The 13th Michigan went into camp at Kalamazoo soon after. His physical description from the regimental muster book says he was twenty-three years of age and five feet, six inches tall and had a light complexion, brown hair and brown eyes. He could not read or write. He was mustered into service on January 17, 1862, by Captain Arad Balch.

The 13th Michigan Infantry left Kalamazoo on February 12, 1862, and according to the Record of Service of the 13th Michigan Infantry, arrived at Pittsburgh Landing in Shiloh, Tennessee, on April 7, 1862, where it supported General Grant and his army following the battle. The regiment then marched to Stevenson, Alabama, where it helped to build fortifications, as there was a large amount of supplies for the army located there. The account continues, "General Buell…left the Thirteenth with a small garrison to hold Stevenson. Here Colonel Shoemaker [commanding officer of the 13th] received a series of orders, one to evacuate the post and fall back to Dechard, and the next to remain and defend the place to the last extremity."

It was during the 13th's evacuation of the garrison that Cyrus was taken prisoner by the rebels on August 26, 1862. He was soon released, and he was sent to Carver Hospital at Washington, D.C., where it was later reported to the regiment that he died. But Cyrus was actually still among the living and was sent back to Michigan.

Apparently, Cyrus was eager to get back into the fighting, because on October 1, 1862, he enlisted as a private in Company K, 6th Michigan Cavalry, at the village of Thornapple in Barry County. He was mustered into the regiment on October 13. The 6th Cavalry went into camp at Grand Rapids and left the state on December 10, 1862, headed for Washington, D.C. It would eventually be assigned to the Michigan Cavalry Brigade, along with the 1st, 5th and 7th Michigan Cavalry Regiments, and placed under the command of a young upstart of a general from Monroe, Michigan, named George Armstrong Custer.

The 6th Michigan fought in several battles and skirmishes, including Hunterstown, Gettysburg, the Wilderness, Cold Harbor, Cedar Creek and Yellow Tavern. In February 1864, members of the 6th Cavalry were involved in what is known as Kilpatrick's Raid. General Judson Kilpatrick, the overall commander of the cavalry, ordered a raid into Richmond, Virginia, the capital of the confederacy. Two hundred men were selected from the brigade, and one of those men was Cyrus Welch. The raid did not go off as planned, and on March 1, Cyrus was captured for the second time during the war. The capture took place at Hyman Bridge on the outskirts of Richmond. Cyrus was confined at Richmond and most likely held at the notorious Belle Isle Prison, as it is well documented that many members of the 6th Michigan Cavalry were there. He was released on May 8, 1864, at City Point, Virginia, and returned to his regiment. Cyrus was discharged for disability on June 28, 1865, at Annapolis, Maryland.

Grave of Cyrus Welch, GAR lot, Riverside Cemetery. *Photo by the author.*

Cyrus returned home to Michigan, where he courted and married Miss Mary Bashinler at Caledonia, on March 15, 1869. The two moved to Middleville in northern Barry County. His four years of service, including the two times he was confined in a Confederate prison, took a toll. He gave up farming and began working as a common laborer, taking jobs when he could get them.

Cyrus applied for a pension for disability from the government on August

3, 1884, but it was denied. Perhaps the strain of his service, his inability to earn much of a living and being unable to collect a pension contributed to his eventual breakdown.

Cyrus was admitted to the Michigan Soldiers' Home at Grand Rapids on June 4, 1889. He stated on the application for admittance that he suffered from paralysis. Apparently, Cyrus was suffering mental issues, because just eight weeks later, he "went insane," becoming so violent that his own safety, the safety of the other residents of the Soldiers' Home and his family was a concern. He was taken by the Barry County sheriff and placed in the county jail at Hastings, until the probate court found him legally unable to function in society. The court ordered him admitted to the asylum. Cyrus was somehow able to escape his cell and made his way out of the jail. He was again caught, and Sheriff Shriner managed to deliver him to the asylum in Kalamazoo on August 1, 1889. One can only speculate if this breakdown and the symptoms of paralysis would now be classified as post-traumatic stress.

Cyrus died in the asylum on January 31, 1892, of general paralysis. No one came to claim the remains, so he was buried at the soldier's lot in Riverside by the GAR.

Ezra S. Scott

Ezra Samuel Scott was born on April 5, 1842, at Bucyrus, Crawford County, Ohio, to Joseph and Phoebe (Stanclift) Scott. The 1860 census shows Ezra living in Decatur, Michigan, working as a shoemaker. In the fall of 1861, he made his way to Adrian, Michigan, a distance of 129 miles, (most likely along the Chicago Road, now U.S. 12), where he enlisted in Company H, 4th Michigan Infantry, on October 8, at the age of nineteen. The descriptive book says that Ezra was five feet, eight inches tall and had a dark complexion, gray eyes and dark hair. It did not mention anything about his passionate determination to fight to preserve the Union.

The 4th Michigan was commanded by Colonel Dwight Woodbury. The regiment left the state on June 25, 1861, and headed for Washington, D.C., where it was posted in the defenses of the capital. It was first engaged in battle with the rebels at New Bridge, Virginia, on May 24, 1862, and Hanover Courthouse, Virginia, on May 27, 1862. During this time, Ezra became disabled, either by sickness or wound, it is not known which. He was discharged at Detroit for disability on June 26, 1862. Seven months later,

Ezra reenlisted in the army at Ypsilanti, Michigan, on January 6, 1863, this time as a corporal in Company D of the 1st Michigan Sharpshooters.

Corporal Scott's new regiment had initially been organized at Kalamazoo but moved to Dearborn to complete the process. It was while at Dearborn that Company D, along with Companies A, B, C, E and F, were sent to Indianapolis, Indiana, to assist in the defense against Confederate general John Hunt Morgan and his cavalry to keep them from moving any farther north. The Sharpshooters were able to successfully defend the town of North Vernon, and Morgan and his men moved into Ohio. It was there that Morgan and his men were captured. The six companies of sharpshooters returned to Dearborn to finalize the organization of the regiment.

In August of that year, Ezra and his comrades were on their way to Chicago to guard the Confederate prisoners located at Camp Douglas. On March 17, 1864, the regiment was sent to Annapolis, Maryland, where it was assigned to the 9th Army Corps under Major General Ambrose E. Burnside. Just a few weeks later, the 1st Michigan Sharpshooters found itself in heavy fighting in the most God forsaken place in Virginia—the Wilderness. The regiment fought for two hellish days, where the troops sustained the first of many casualties. Ezra was one of them.

In Raymond J. Herek's book *These Men Have Seen Hard Service*, Ezra is mentioned on page 123 in a description of the fighting the sharpshooters endured. Ezra was shot in the left shoulder, fracturing the shoulder blade. He was permanently out of action. For the second time, Ezra was discharged at Detroit for disability on December 17, 1864. His passionate determination had been frustrated by a Confederate bullet.

If Ezra thought he had seen a lot of the country during the war, he would continue his adventure after it. Ezra's wound proved to be a lingering reminder of his service. He applied for a soldier's pension on March 12, 1865, and received twelve dollars per month for the next forty years.

About that same time, he married his first wife, Almira, and they resettled in Leslie, Ingham County, Michigan. To this union were born three children, Elmer, Edward and Elizabeth. Almira died in 1874. Ezra,

Grave of Ezra S. Scott, GAR lot, Riverside Cemetery. *Photo by the author.*

perhaps wanting his children to grow up with a mother and, perhaps taking his physical condition into account, married Rose A. Chelsey on April 7, 1875. Ezra and Rose had three more children, Anna, Lorenzo and Arvada.

This is where Ezra's adventure continues. By 1880, he had moved his family to Clay County, Iowa. He took up farming and tried to make a go of it. We can assume it didn't work out, because on March 31, 1883, Ezra joined the Zach Chandler Post No. 35, Grand Army of the Republic, at South Haven, Van Buren County, Michigan. Perhaps he didn't find Iowa to be what he really wanted. Ezra and Rose soon moved to Kalamazoo and resided at 520 Winstead Street. This street no longer exists, as it was removed to make room for the Bronson Hospital parking lot.

Ezra died on September 23, 1905, at the age of sixty-three of heart disease and neuralgia, a condition that causes intense pain along the course of a nerve. He was buried on September 25. The *Kalamazoo Gazette* said of the funeral, in part, "Some of his comrades bore his remains to their final resting place. His casket was draped with the stars and stripes, to which he had been so loyal."

Ezra's passionate determination was well known, even at his death.

Thomas W. Warren

"Tom Warren, an old soldier, night watchman, detective and one of the best-known men in Kalamazoo, fell dead at his home, 820 Jackson Street, at 8 o'clock Tuesday morning."

This is the first line of the obituary for a man who, at several times in his adult life, was scorned for his behavior and ridiculed for his methods of police work. There is no question that in at least one instance, if really true, he could have been arrested for watching people through their windows at night instead of keeping them safe.

Tom Warren was born on March 4, 1841, in New York, the son of Robert and Eliza Warren. By 1860, Tom was living in Kalamazoo, and enlisted in Company F, 19th Michigan Infantry, as a wagoner. He was mustered into service on September 5, 1862, and was discharged for disability at Detroit on December 23, 1864.

Tom married Elizabeth "Lizzie" Luce in 1865, and they had two sons, Albert, born in 1867, and Edward, born in 1868. Tom first found work as a drayman, someone who delivered goods on a horse-drawn, flat-bed wagon.

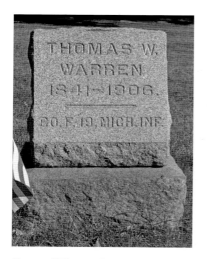

Grave of Thomas W. Warren, GAR lot, Riverside Cemetery. *Photo by the author.*

In 1884, he is mentioned in the *Kalamazoo Gazette* as a "special policeman," working for the village of Kalamazoo. The article also mentions that he was brought up on charges for assaulting police officer Henry Boekeloo at police headquarters on September 23, 1884. The charges state that Tom "did assault Policeman Henry Boekeloo, and threw him down, injuring him severely in the leg." A supplemental report from Marshal Stephen H. Wattles acknowledges that Boekeloo was drunk on duty several times and he was "quarrelsome and troublesome…particularly toward Special Policeman Thomas Warren." On October 22, the *Gazette* reported that Tom had been "fined $25.00 and costs for assaulting Policeman Boekeloo." He was also removed as a special policeman. Tom's troubles had only begun.

In an editorial in the August 7, 1887 edition of the *Kalamazoo Gazette*, there appears a column titled "The Man in the Moon," in which Tom Warren is described as nothing more than a peeping Tom, a reprobate who "has conducted himself in a manner that richly merits a coat of tar and feathers as his punishment." The article is a scathing recital of actions that Tom had supposedly carried out—watching ladies getting ready for bed through their windows, watching ladies in a dress shop trying on dresses and making inquiries about two young ladies who were visiting Kalamazoo as to what their business was in town. The paper accused Tom of looking into this for his own edification to "appease his appetite for scandal." It is clear that someone at the *Gazette* did not like Tom Warren.

Tom's opportunity to redeem himself came in 1893, when a murder took place in the city. Louis Schilling, the owner of a meat market at 118 Portage Street, was attacked in his establishment. He was bludgeoned, and his throat was cut from ear to ear. Over the next several months, there were many suspects arrested, questioned and ultimately let go. For several years, Tom put all he had into the investigation.

The personal attacks on Tom resumed on June 12, 1894, when he was escorting an individual who was to be admitted to the Kalamazoo Asylum, by order of the judge of probate. At the corner of Main and Burdick Street, the man got away from Tom, and the chase was on. The *Gazette* gave a detailed account of what happened next:

> *He* [the escapee], *turned east at Bush and Patterson and swam the river. He ran towards the south and picked up an axe somewhere. At the old fairground he chopped down a barbed wire fence and went into a field and got a horse belonging to a German family living in the neighborhood. The owners of the animal started on the run after him and before they reached him he jumped from the horse and ran towards the railroad track. He got there just as the south-bound passenger train was due and by waving his hat, handkerchief and axe succeeded in stopping it long enough to jump on.*

The article continued, describing how when the train reached Schoolcraft the man began breaking out the windows of the car with the axe. He was taken into custody by Deputy Sheriff Gill and eventually taken to the asylum. One can only imagine the bruise left on Tom's ego.

Tom never let go of the Schilling case. The January 27, 1899 edition of the *Kalamazoo Evening News* ran the following story:

> *In Prosecutors Hands*
> *Detective Warren Has Placed Testimony in Schilling Murder Case*
>
> *Tom Warren, the Kalamazoo Sleuth, who has worked untiringly for six years, trying to obtain a clue to the murder of the Portage Street meat market man, Louis Schilling, recently stated that he was positive the fate of the murderers depended upon the discretion of a wreck of humanity, who has been filed with wiskey [sic] every day in order to keep him from telling all he knows. Warren thinks that a great mistake was made in not barricading the vicinity in which the murder was committed and beginning a careful research immediately for evidence. It is believed that the deed was perpetrated for the purpose of obtaining money, but as only $35 was secured, the act was all the more revolting. Warren has handed a pile of sworn testimony to Prosecuting Attorney Master to be filed away. Many of the witnesses are dead and a number of changes have occurred to make the affair still more complicated.*

Tom Warren died of a stroke on Tuesday, September 11, 1906, and was buried at the GAR lot in Riverside. The murder was never solved.

William Hawthorne

Born in Hillsborough, County Down, Ireland, in 1838, William immigrated to the United States in his youth. He left his parents in Ireland, perhaps like so many, to seek the opportunity for a better life. He could not write and probably could not read, either.

When the War of the Rebellion commenced in April 1861, William was living in Detroit. He traveled to Kalamazoo, where he enlisted on May 10, 1861, as a private in Company K of the 2nd Michigan Infantry. He was twenty-three years old. William served under Captain Charles S. May, also of Kalamazoo, who commanded the company. The regiment was mustered into the federal service on May 25, 1861.

The 2nd Michigan was part of the Army of the Potomac and was soon engaged in the Peninsula Campaign in Virginia, under Major General George Brinton McClellan. William was wounded in the right leg at the Siege of Yorktown, Virginia, in April 1862. Later, the regiment was transferred to the western theater of the war.

Even a battle wound would not dissuade William from doing his duty for his adopted country, for on December 31, 1863, at Blain's Crossroads, Tennessee, he reenlisted for another three years, or the duration of the war. He was mustered the next day, January 1, 1864.

William was promoted to corporal on September 16, 1864. He must have been either very proud, very nervous or both. He was taking on more responsibility, got to wear two blue stripes on each of his sleeves and would receive more pay. (Privates earned thirteen dollars per month and a corporal sixteen dollars per month.)

William was captured and held as a prisoner of war at Salisbury, North Carolina, from October 1864 to May 1865. While incarcerated for those seven months, he contracted scurvy and chronic diarrhea, which plagued him for the rest of his life.

After his release from the POW camp, William returned to the 2nd Michigan and was discharged with his regiment at Delaney House in Washington, D.C., on July 28, 1865.

William returned to Michigan and resided in Pontiac in Oakland County. He never married. He worked as a laborer for the next twenty years, until his health began to fail him, and he was unable to care for himself any longer. On November 30, 1889, he was admitted to the Michigan Soldier's Home at Grand Rapids. For reasons unknown, he was discharged from the home on April 25, 1891. It is possible that he went back to Pontiac. Starting

Stories of the Veterans

Grave of William Hawthorne, GAR lot, Riverside Cemetery. *Photo by the author.*

around 1890, William began to receive a disability pension in the amount of six dollars per month, due to the wound in his right leg.

William applied for readmission to the Soldier's Home in March 1899. Just thirteen months later, on April 21, 1900, he was sent to the Kalamazoo Asylum for the Insane. In the days following, his personal effects were sent from Grand Rapids via American Express to the asylum. The package included his "clothing, shaving outfit, trinkets, etc." William died at the asylum the day after Christmas in 1901. The cause of death was listed as cerebral softening. He was sixty-three years old.

According to the obituary in the *Kalamazoo Telegraph*, an attempt was made to locate friends or relatives, but none could be found. The funeral was held at Truesdale's Undertaking Rooms, with Orcutt Post No. 79 in charge of the services. William was buried at the Grand Army of the Republic lot in Section R on December 28. It was fitting that the veterans took care of William's remains and lay him down to his final rest, because they understood.

They understood that William had taken part in the entire war, from its very beginning to its very end. He had left the security of home and enlisted to preserve the Union just a few weeks after the rebels fired on Fort Sumter. He experienced both defeat and victory on the battlefield and was promoted in rank. William had been wounded in battle, captured and held as a prisoner of war. He suffered malnourishment and disease, experienced long marches in the summer's heat and the winter's cold. William had seen his friends die. He was consumed by the jubilation of the end of the war and the sadness of Lincoln's assassination. William had also received an honorable discharge. He had done it all. For four long years, William had sacrificed for his country—he was truly a veteran.

A headstone was finally placed on his grave in 2001, one hundred years after his death.

Epilogue

Moses and Frances Hodgman lived out their years in Climax. Moses died in 1881, at the age of seventy-six. His wife, Frances, would follow him in death in 1896. They are buried at the family plot in Climax's Prairie Home Cemetery.

Frank Hodgman became a civil engineer and served as the Kalamazoo County surveyor. He also became a poet, publishing a book of his work in 1898, titled *The Wondering Singer and His Songs and Other Poems*. He married Miss Florence B. Cumings. Florence died in 1888 and is buried in Galesburg. Frank died in Galesburg in 1907 and is buried with his parents in Climax. It is not certain what became of Charles.

While serving in the 7th Michigan Infantry, Sam was promoted to first lieutenant on September 2, 1862. On September 17, Sam and the 7th Michigan found themselves in action at Sharpsburg, Maryland, in the bloody Battle of Antietam. Sam was wounded in action but recovered. He was promoted to captain on June 22, 1863, just before his regiment fought at Gettysburg, participating in the repulse of Pickett's Charge on the front lines on July 3. Due to his wounds, he was honorably discharged on March 1, 1864.

Sam, too, became an engineer, working with his brother Frank. In 1885, Sam moved to Haines City, Florida. He joined the Episcopal church, studied for the ministry and was ordained on December 27, 1894. The Reverend Samuel Hodgman died on April 1, 1900, and is buried at Forest Hill Cemetery in Haines City.

Appendix

Kalamazoo County Roll of Honor

The following list was originally compiled by several citizens of Kalamazoo County in the 1990s and contained the names of those citizens of the county who "gave the last full measure." From this list, a plaque was created and currently hangs in Veterans' Memorial Hall in the county courthouse. Every year, the names of all Kalamazoo County war dead are read at the Memorial Day ceremonies held in Veterans' Memorial Garden at Riverside Cemetery. This list appears courtesy of the Kalamazoo Detachment No. 879 of the Marine Corps League.

Current research by the author into the names on this list has resulted in discovering that a few of the individuals on the list in fact survived the war. Those have been removed from this list. The spelling of some of the names has been corrected through research comparing the 1850 and 1860 U.S. Censuses and the record of service published by the State of Michigan. Three names not previously on the list have been added. For the purpose of this book, the author has researched and added the rank and regiment in which the soldier served. The primary sources for verification are *History of Kalamazoo County*, published in 1880 by Everts and Abbott, and the *Michigan Soldiers and Sailors Individual Records*, published by the State of Michigan in 1905, from the records of the Adjutant General's Office, Lansing. This series of forty-six volumes and an index book are known in the Civil War

Appendix

community as the Brown Books, as the bindings are dark brown with black letters. The full set can be accessed at the Hathi Trust Digital Library (babel.hathitrust.org), and an original set can be found in the Archives of Western Michigan University.

Charles Adair, Company F, 19th Michigan Infantry
Charles Adams, Company H, 44th Illinois Infantry
Christopher Alkinback, Company I, 13th Michigan Infantry
Charles H. Allcott, Sergeant, Company D, 17th Michigan Infantry
George F. Allen, Company L, 1st Michigan Cavalry
George W. Allen, Company E, 25th Michigan Infantry
William E. Allen, Company G, 13th Michigan Infantry
Stephen M. Andrews, Company G, 11th Michigan Infantry
Henry Andrus, Company H, 7th Michigan Cavalry
John Andrus, Company K, 1st Michigan Cavalry
Turner Archie, Company C, 1st Michigan Colored Infantry
John P. Austin, Company G, 11th Michigan Infantry
John S. Austin, Sergeant, Company M, 11th Michigan Cavalry
Levi Austin, Company G, 11th Michigan Infantry
Benjamin F. Axtell, Company L, 5th Michigan Cavalry
Isaac Babcock, Company H, 44th Illinois Infantry
Henry Bacon, Sergeant Company I, 11th Michigan Cavalry
Barton Bailey, Company E, 25th Michigan Infantry
George Barter, Company E, 3rd Michigan Cavalry
Orrin M. Bartlett, Company M, 1st Michigan Cavalry
William Bates, Company C, 1st Michigan Engineers & Mechanics
James A. Batt, Company H, 7th Michigan Cavalry
William H. Batt, Company L, 6th Michigan Cavalry
Henry Beals, Company C, 70th New York Infantry
Carlos T. Bean, Company K, 19th Michigan Infantry
Dexter Beard, Company F, 11th Michigan Infantry
George Beck, Company H, 1st Michigan Cavalry
Merchant S. Beebe, Company C, 6th Michigan Infantry
Charles E. Benson, Company I, 7th Michigan Infantry
Amiron Bidgood, Company L, 1st Michigan Cavalry
Alanson Billings, Company H, 25th Michigan Infantry
Oliver B. Bingham, Company H, 44th Illinois Infantry
Oscar A. Birdsell, Corporal, Company C, 13th Michigan Infantry
Charles L. Bissell, Lieutenant, 12th Michigan Infantry

Appendix

David Blanchard, Company C, 1st Michigan Sharpshooters
Simon F. Blanchard, Company D, 17th Michigan Infantry
James F. Bloomer, Company C, 6th Michigan Infantry
Samuel Bonner, Company H, 12th Michigan Infantry
John Boughton, Company K, 8th Michigan Cavalry
Eli D. Bowen, Company H, 11th Michigan Cavalry
William H. Bowen, Company H, 7th Michigan Cavalry
Stephan D. Bowerman, Company G, 13th Michigan Infantry
George Bowman, Company H, 44th Illinois Infantry
Francis Brierly, Company H, 13th Michigan Infantry
John E. Briggs, Sergeant, Company H, 7th Michigan Cavalry
Gottlieb E. Brodbeck, Company A, 6th Michigan Infantry
Eugene H. Bronson, Company C, 4th Michigan Cavalry
Henry Brown, Company A, 13th Michigan Infantry
Horace W. Brown, Company B, 12th Michigan Infantry
William H. Brownell, Corporal, Company L, 11th Michigan Cavalry
John C. Buck, Company A, 12th Michigan Infantry
John E. Bunbury, Company F, 19th Michigan Infantry
John Burchet, Company F, 3rd Michigan Cavalry
George Burchette, Company K, 19th Michigan Infantry
Charles E. Burdick, Company H, 25th Michigan Infantry
Caroden S. Burge, Corporal, Company K, 2nd Michigan Infantry
Abner H. Burson, Company L, 5th Michigan Cavalry
Joseph Burson, Company L, 5th Michigan Cavalry
Elijah P. Bush, Company K, 13th Michigan Infantry
William Callahan, Company K, 2nd Michigan Infantry
Edgar N. Camp, Company M, 3rd Michigan Cavalry
Myron C. Capell, Company H, 44th Illinois Infantry
Thomas Carney, Company I, 13th Michigan Infantry
Manville E. Carpenter, Company H, 13th Michigan Infantry
William Carpenter, Company I, 2nd Michigan Cavalry
Moses Carr, Battery I, 1st Michigan Light Artillery
Henry B. Carrier, Company I, 2nd Michigan Infantry
George W. Carter, Company K, 1st Michigan Engineers & Mechanics
Judson W. Carter, Company K, 1st Michigan Engineers & Mechanics
Samuel Case, Company L, 5th Michigan Cavalry
David Casselman, Company F, 8th Michigan Cavalry
William H. Casselman, Company F, 8th Michigan Cavalry
William T. Casselman, Company M, 8th Michigan Cavalry

Appendix

Adam Castelan, Company M, 10th Michigan Cavalry
John Castner, Company L, 5th Michigan Cavalry
William E. Chaffee, Company I, 17th Michigan Infantry
William Chambers, Company G, 8th Michigan Cavalry
Alfred Chandler, Company F, 8th Michigan Cavalry
Albert B. Chapman, Company C, 6th Michigan Infantry
Albert Chase, Company L, 6th Michigan Cavalry
William H. Chase, Company H, 44th Illinois Infantry
Myron Cole, Company D, 11th Michigan Cavalry
George W. Collins, Company C, 13th Michigan Infantry
George C. Colton, Company G, 1st Michigan Engineers & Mechanics
Jonas Compton, Company C, 6th Michigan Infantry
Edwin Conkright, Company H, 44th Illinois Infantry
Joseph Cook, Company I, 2nd Michigan Infantry
Samuel Cook, Company H, 25th Michigan Infantry
Frank Corbyn, Second Lieutenant, Company I, 3rd Michigan Cavalry
Albert Corey, Company H, 44th Illinois Infantry
James Cornell, Company H, 7th Michigan Cavalry
John C. Crofoot, Company E, 13th Michigan Infantry
Samuel W. Crooks, Company H, 25th Michigan Infantry
George Cross, Company I, 1st Michigan Cavalry
Manilus Cross, Company L, 5th Michigan Cavalry
Aaron A. Culver, Company E, 9th Michigan Infantry
John W. Cummins, Company L, 5th Michigan Cavalry
Edward A. Curtenius, Captain, 15th U.S. Infantry
John A. Davis, Company F, 19th Michigan Infantry
Joseph Davison, Company G, 1st Michigan Cavalry
Perry Deforrest, Company G, 11th Michigan Infantry
Stephan B. DeLano, Company F, 3rd Michigan Cavalry
Horace E. Demarest, Company L, Merrill Horse
Phillip Demarest, Company L, Merrill Horse
William Deming, Company I, 7th Michigan Infantry
Cortland J. Dennis, Company F, 19th Michigan Infantry
Joseph DeWaters, Company E, 13th Michigan Infantry
Orville H. DeWaters, Company H, 13th Michigan Infantry
Stephan Dillingham, Company K, 2nd Michigan Cavalry
Nelson Dingman, Company K, 6th Michigan Infantry
Peter D. Dingman, Company K, 19th Michigan Infantry
John Dixson, Company L, 5th Michigan Cavalry

Appendix

Alaski Dolson, Company I, 17th Michigan Infantry
Leonard G.M. Dorr, Company G, 13th Michigan Infantry
John F. Droman, Company F, 19th Michigan Infantry
Milton Drummond, Company D, 13th Michigan Infantry
Edwin S. Drury, Company C, 4th Michigan Cavalry
Robert Duncan, Company L, 1st Michigan Cavalry
William N. Dunsha, Company F, 19th Michigan Infantry
Benjamin F. Earl, Company L, 6th Michigan Cavalry
William Echtenaw, Company K, 19th Michigan Infantry
Rueben Edmonds, Battery G, 1st Michigan Light Artillery
Richard H. Eldred, Company K, 2nd Michigan Infantry
James Elkins, Company L, 6th Michigan Cavalry
Chauncey Evans, Company D, 17th Michigan Infantry
Horatio C. Failing, Company C, 28th Michigan Infantry
Henry J. Fairfield, Company M, 11th Michigan Cavalry
David Farnsworth, Company I, 7th Michigan Infantry
Joseph Fay, Company G, 6th Michigan Infantry
John Fenn, Company E, 25th Michigan Infantry
James Ferris, Company H, 5th Michigan Infantry
Benjamin F. Filkins, Company H, 44th Illinois Infantry
Jeremiah Filkins, Company H, 44th Illinois Infantry
Miles Finch, Company A, 13th Michigan Infantry
David Finehout, Company L, 5th Michigan Cavalry
Frank Fisher, Sergeant, Company I, 17th Michigan Infantry
Abram R. Flint, Company C, 147th Illinois Infantry
Thomas Flynn, Company F, 3rd Michigan Cavalry
Irving B. Follet, Company I, 1st Michigan Cavalry
Carey Forbes, Company I, 1st Michigan Cavalry
Benjamin C. Freeman, Company F, 1st Michigan Sharpshooters
Addison French, Company L, 5th Michigan Cavalry
Albert E. Fuller, Company F, 11th Michigan Cavalry
Oscar E. Fuller, Company F, 11th Michigan Infantry
Edward Funnel, Company H, Merrill Horse
William Furney, Company F, 19th Michigan Infantry
George Galligan, Company I, 17th Michigan Infantry
Richard H. Gardner, Company I, 2nd Michigan Infantry
Burr Garrett, Company C, 6th Michigan Infantry
George A. Gay, Company K, 13th Michigan Infantry
Allen Gayton, Company B, 1st Michigan Colored Infantry

Appendix

James M. Geddes, Sergeant, Company L, 6th Michigan Cavalry
Elisha Geer, Company K, 12th Michigan Infantry
Leonard Gibbon, Company K, 19th Michigan Infantry
Anson J. Gilbert, Company D, 6th Michigan Infantry
Lawrence Gorman, Company G, 1st Michigan Infantry
William A. Green, Company F, 19th Michigan Infantry
Reuben Griggs, Company F, 11th Michigan Infantry
Reuben Gromman, Company B, 4th Michigan Cavalry
Martin L. Guy, Company E, 1st Michigan Colored Infantry
James E. Hall, Company F, 6th Michigan Infantry
Walter S. Hamilton, Company L, Merrill Horse
William B. Harger, Company B, 12th Michigan Infantry
George A. Harns, Company L, Merrill Horse
George L. Harrington, Company L, 6th Michigan Cavalry
Elijah D. Harris, Company I, 13th Michigan Infantry
Spencer Harrison, Company L, 6th Michigan Cavalry
James Harvey, Company K, 2nd Michigan Infantry
Charles H. Haskall, Company D, 17th Michigan Infantry
Henry H. Hathaway, Company E, 25th Michigan Infantry
James D. Hathaway, Company H, 11th Michigan Cavalry
John G. Hathaway, Company K, 30th Michigan Infantry
James B. Hawkes, Company I, 7th Michigan Infantry
Charles B. Hayden, Lieutenant Colonel, 2nd Michigan Infantry
Theodore C. Henshaw, Corporal, Company F, 3rd Michigan Cavalry
Horace Hewitt, Company F, 6th Michigan Infantry
George W. Hicks, Company E, 25th Michigan Infantry
William Hildebrand, Company E, 12th Michigan Infantry
Edwin E. Hill, Company H, 25th Michigan Infantry
William Hilts, Company G, 1st Michigan Engineers & Mechanics
Robert Hooper, Company G, 13th Michigan Infantry
William Hooper, Company F, 19th Michigan Infantry
John Hopkins, Company F, 11th Michigan Cavalry
Augustus House, Company I, 2nd Michigan Cavalry
Samuel H. Hovey, Company D, 17th Michigan Infantry
Francis M. Howe, Company A, 13th Michigan Infantry
William Huggitt, Company H, 44th Illinois Infantry
Samuel Hunt, Company D, 17th Michigan Infantry
Ralph Hymen, Company I, 1st Michigan Cavalry
Norman W. Ingersoll, Company L, 5th Michigan Cavalry

Appendix

Edwin J. Innis, Corporal, Company L, 6th Michigan Cavalry
Stephan H. Irwin, Sergeant, Company I, 1st Michigan Cavalry
George N. Ives, Company K, 1st Michigan Engineers & Mechanics
Dego Jeffers, Company A, 35th Illinois Infantry
Elwood Jennings, Company B, 12th Michigan Infantry
Edward M. Jewett, Company B, 6th Michigan Infantry
Moses E. Kellett, Company E, 25th Michigan Infantry
James C. Kennicut, Company L, 5th Michigan Cavalry
Henry B. Kercher, Battery H, 1st Michigan Light Artillery
George W. Keyser, Sergeant, Company F, 8th Michigan Cavalry
Jesse Kimball, Company B, 13th Michigan Infantry
John D. B. Kline, Corporal, Company C, 6th Michigan Infantry
Orrin C. Knapp, Company C, 70th New York Infantry
Vine Knapp, Company H, 7th Michigan Cavalry
Melvin Knappen, Company G, 13th Michigan Infantry
Haven Knight, Company B, 11th Michigan Infantry
William Koster, Company A, 2nd Michigan Cavalry
James M. Langs, Company F, 19th Michigan Infantry
Nathaniel Lanphere, Corporal, Company H, 121st New York Infantry
Chester E. Lee, Company E, 12th Michigan Infantry
John W. Lee, Company H, 25th Michigan Infantry
Alexander O. Leeper, Sergeant, Company K, 19th Michigan Infantry
Henry Leland, Company B, 6th Michigan Infantry
August Lemcool, Company F, 3rd Michigan Cavalry
Peter Lemcool, Company F, 1st Michigan Engineers & Mechanics
Theodore Lemon, Company K, 2nd Michigan Infantry
Benjamin F. Leslie, Company C, 13th Michigan Infantry
William Leslie, Sergeant, Company F, 11th Michigan Cavalry
Franklin F. Lewis, Company I, 2nd Michigan Cavalry
Jacob Louck, Company F, 19th Michigan Infantry
Everett W. Lusk, Sergeant Major, 1st Michigan Cavalry
Caleb Lyndon, Company H, 12th Michigan Infantry
Barney Manion, Company K, 19th Michigan Infantry
Eugene W. Martin, Company H, 7th Michigan Cavalry
George F. Martin, Company E, 25th Michigan Infantry
Zala Martin, Company K, 19th Michigan Infantry
George P. Mason, Capatin, Company I, 11th Michigan Cavalry
James Mathers, Captain, Company L, 6th Michigan Cavalry
William H. McClary, Corporal, Company H, 7th Michigan Cavalry

Appendix

Michael T. McEnnis, Sergeant, Company A, 17th Michigan Infantry
James McMann, Company C, 70th New York Infantry
Daniel E. McMartin, Company D, 17th Michigan Infantry
Benjamin Merrick, Company E, 28th Michigan Infantry
David C. Merrill, Company H, 1st Michigan Infantry
Daniel F. Miller, Sergeant, Company L, 5th Michigan Cavalry
Harry Mills, Company H, 7th Michigan Cavalry
Asa S. Monroe, Corporal, Company K, 13th Michigan Infantry
Alexander Moored, Company G, 13th Michigan Infantry
Jared Morton, Company L, 6th Michigan Cavalry
Quincy P. Morton, Company F, 8th Michigan Cavalry
John Mowry, Company L, 5th Michigan Cavalry
Alanson W. Munger, Company C, 4th Michigan Cavalry
Edwin Newell, Company H, 1st Michigan Infantry
John Newell, Company I, 2nd Michigan Infantry
Milton A. Newton, Company E, 13th Michigan Infantry
William H. Nichols, Sergeant, Company H, 7th Michigan Cavalry
Charles R. Nightingale, Company K, 13th Michigan Infantry
Lewis C. Northrop, Company I, 19th Michigan Infantry
John Nysse, Company G, 13th Michigan Infantry
Matthew O'Brien, Company A, 5th Michigan Cavalry
Patrick O'Maley, Company H, 44th Illinois Infantry
Walter T. Orr, Company A, 13th Michigan Infantry
Charles A. Orton, Company A, 1st Michigan Engineers & Mechanics
Scott Osborn, Company E, 13th Michigan Infantry
Calvin Osmer, Company G, 1st Michigan Engineers & Mechanics
Ralph Overracker, Company H, 44th Illinois Infantry
Andrew J. Overton, Company I, 1st Michigan Cavalry
Benjamin Owen, Company F, 19th Michigan Infantry
John L. Palmer, Company H, 7th Michigan Cavalry
Walter Parish, Company E, 25th Michigan Infantry
Henry I. Parker, Corporal, Company C, 1st U.S. Sharpshooters
Chauncy Parmalee, Company M, 8th Michigan Cavalry
Charles A. Parsons, Company D, 25th Michigan Infantry
Stephan Patterson, 1st Lieutenant, Company I, 7th Michigan Infantry
Charles Pennell, Company F, 8th Michigan Cavalry
George Pennells, Company F, 19th Michigan Infantry
Noah Purdue, Company C, 1st Michigan Colored Infantry
Reuben F. Perkins, Company L, Merrill Horse

Appendix

George C. Petrie, Company D, 17th Michigan Infantry
William Petrie, Company E, 1st Michigan Sharpshooters
Thomas Phelan, Sergeant, Company L, 5th Michigan Cavalry
Alexander B. Philow Jr., Company I, 13th Michigan Infantry
Elijah Pitts, Company K, 13th Michigan Infantry
Mortimer L. Pond, Company H, 30th Michigan Infantry
Charles J. Porter, Sergeant, Company K, 2nd Michigan Infantry
Gideon E. Portman, Company K, 19th Michigan Infantry
Homer B. Potter, Sergeant, Company I, 17th Michigan Infantry
William W. Potter, Corporal, Company I, 17th Michigan Infantry
Alfred F. Powell, Company D, 17th Michigan Infantry
Lafayette Price, Company G, 1st Michigan Cavalry
Milo Price, Corporal, Company F, 8th Michigan Infantry
Caleb A. Prouty, Company K, 6th Michigan Infantry
Orson Prouty, Battery C, 1st Michigan Light Artillery
Wallace Prouty, Company E, 5th Michigan Cavalry
Charles G. Pursell, First Lieutenant, Company H, 19th Michigan Infantry
James B. Quick, Company H, 44th Illinois Infantry
Henry M. Reasner, Company H, 7th Michigan Cavalry
James M. Reese, Company K, 2nd Michigan Infantry
Chauncy Reeve, Company F, 19th Michigan Infantry
James Reynolds, First Lieutenant, Company K, 7th Michigan Infantry
William H. Richards, Company H, 7th Michigan Cavalry
Allen Rickard, Company H, 25th Michigan Infantry
Timothy Riley, Company H, 25th Michigan Infantry
Isaac Robbins, Company F, 3rd Michigan Cavalry
Henry P. Robinson, Company L, 5th Michigan Cavalry
Joseph J. Robinson, Company D, Western Sharpshooters
Floyd Rockwell, Company L, 5th Michigan Cavalry
Spencer A. Rowley, Company A, 6th Michigan Infantry
Eli Russell, Sergeant, Company I, 2nd Michigan Cavalry
Ulysses D. Russell, Color Sergeant, Company I, 2nd Michigan Infantry
John Schoonover, Company C, 1st U.S. Sharpshooters
Allen Sears, Company K, 2nd Michigan Infantry
Abraham Sebring, Company C, 4th Michigan Cavalry
Edward M. Severance, Company C, 6th Michigan Infantry
Frank Seymour, Corporal, Company C, 2nd Michigan Cavalry
Marshal Seymour, Company I, 7th Michigan Infantry
Charles F. Shafer, Company A, 7th Michigan Cavalry

APPENDIX

Bruce A. Shaver, Corporal, Company F, 19th Michigan Infantry
Samuel M. Shaver, Company F, 19th Michigan Infantry
Francis H. Shaw, Company K, 2nd Michigan Infantry
George A. Sheldon, Second Lieutenant, Company I, 1st U.S. Sharpshooters
George Simmons, Company I, 2nd Michigan Cavalry
Webster I. Skidmore, 8th New York Heavy Artillery
Frederick Smith, Company K, 19th Michigan Infantry
Joseph W. Smith, Company A, 11th Michigan Infantry
Matthew Smith, Company B, 8th Michigan Cavalry
Perry W. Smith, Company H, 7th Michigan Cavalry
Stephan D. Smith, Company H, 7th Michigan Cavalry
Wheaton R. Smith, Company I, 1st Michigan Cavalry
Wilber Smith, Company D, 17th Michigan Infantry
Franklin N. Smithly, Battery F, 1st Michigan Light Artillery
Henry F. Snyder, Company C, 8th Michigan Cavalry
Conrad Somdle, Company H, 1st Michigan Cavalry
John E. Spangler, Battery G, 1st Michigan Light Artillery
Wilbur F. Spaulding, Company I, 6th Michigan Infantry
Joseph E. Sperry, Corporal, Company H, 25th Michigan Infantry
Addison H. Stafford, Sergeant, Company H, 44th Illinois Infantry
Lewis J. Stebbins, Company E, 13th Michigan Infantry
Royal T.A. Stevens, Company F, 19th Michigan Infantry
Charles E. Steward, Company I, 10th Michigan Cavalry
Benjamin V. Stone, Company E, 28th Michigan Infantry
John D. Strickland, Company I, 1st Michigan Cavalry
William C. Swaddle, Sergeant, Company G, 1st Michigan Engineers & Mechanics
Augustus Swartwout, Corporal, Company A, 13th Michigan Infantry
Lorenzo D. Sweet, Company L, 6th Michigan Cavalry
Winfield S. Taber, Sergeant, Company M, 7th Michigan Cavalry
Frank Talman, Company I, 2nd Michigan Cavalry
Dwight Taylor, Company A, 13th Michigan Infantry
Frank Taylor, Company I, 2nd Michigan Infantry
George Taylor, Company H, 13th Michigan Infantry
Rufus D. Thayer, Company H, 44th Illinois Infantry
William J. Thrall, Corporal, Company L, 8th Michigan Cavalry
William S. Tibbitts, Company M, 11th Michigan Cavalry
William Tims, Company I, 6th Michigan Infantry
John Tink, Corporal, Company E, 13th Michigan Infantry
Timothy A. Tower, Company A, 13th Michigan Infantry

Appendix

Benjamin F. Trask, Company B, 5th Michigan Infantry
James G. Traver, Sergeant, Company F, 19th Michigan Infantry
George W. Travis, Sergeant, Company I, 7th Michigan Infantry
William A. Tripp, First Sergeant, Company I, 7th Michigan Infantry
Hiram Tryon, Company G, 13th Michigan Infantry
Eurigan R. Tuttle, Company L, 6th Michigan Cavalry
Henry Upton, Company E, 25th Michigan Infantry
Garrett Van Bree, Company L, 5th Michigan Cavalry
Garrett Vandenburg, Company G, 13th Michigan Infantry
Henry H. Van Est, Company K, 24th Michigan Infantry
William Van Vliet, Company D, Western Sharpshooters
Gerritt Vanzwalanberg, Company K, 2nd Michigan Infantry
Horace A. Varney, Company D, 17th Michigan Infantry
Peter Vealey, Company F, 12th Michigan Infantry
Samuel Vosburg, Company I, 28th Michigan Infantry
Frank E. Walbridge, Captain, Assistant Quartermaster, U.S. Army
George W. Walker, Company H, 25th Michigan Infantry
Octavius Wallace, Corporal, Company I, 2nd Michigan Infantry
Samuel S. Wandell, Company G, 13th Michigan Infantry
Daniel Washburn, Company K, 19th Michigan Infantry
George H. Watkins, Company H, 44th Illinois Infantry
Clement C. Webb, Captain, Company E, 13th Michigan Infantry
Charles L. Weeks, Sergeant, Company I, 17th Michigan Infantry
Frank H. Weeks, Company I, 17th Michigan Infantry
Johnson Wells, Sergeant, Company H, 13th Michigan Infantry
Edward J. Wentworth, Sergeant, Company F, 19th Michigan Infantry
George Wenzel, Company M, 1st Michigan Cavalry
William Westcott, Company I, 7th Michigan Infantry
John Whelan, Company E, 25th Michigan Infantry
Alvah White, Company B, 11th Michigan Infantry
Thomas J. Whiting, Sergeant Major, Company I, 2nd Michigan Infantry
Charles Whitmore, Company E, 28th Michigan Infantry
Cyrus W. Whitney, First Sergeant, Company I, 7th Michigan Infantry
Charles E. Wilkerson, Company I, 2nd Michigan Infantry
Charles Wilson, Company G, 8th Michigan Infantry
George A. Wilson, Company I, 2nd Michigan Infantry
Alphonso Winans, Company, K, 2nd Michigan Infantry
David C. Winegarden, Company F, 8th Michigan Infantry
Isaac J. Winegarden, Company F, 8th Michigan Infantry

Appendix

George Wixsom, Company L, 5th Michigan Cavalry
Henry J. Woodard, Sergeant, Company H, 7th Michigan Cavalry
Andrew J. Woodmansee, Company D, 13th Michigan Infantry
John S. Woodruff, Company L, 11th Michigan Cavalry
Calvin Woolener, Company I, 6th Michigan Infantry
Daniel A. Wright, Company F, 19th Michigan Infantry
Eli Wright, Company D, 12th Michigan Infantry
Thomas C. Wright, Company D, 1st Michigan Sharpshooters
Edger R. Yawger, Company G, 12th Michigan Infantry
James Young, Company G, 13th Michigan Infantry
Amaziah Youngs, Company L, 9th Michigan Cavalry
Nathan H. Youngs, Company F, 3rd Michigan Cavalry

Bibliography

Chapter 1

Kalamazoo in the Antebellum Period

Everts and Abbott. *History of Kalamazoo County Michigan.* Philadelphia: J.B. Lippincott Press, 1880.
Honor Roll of Kalamazoo County. N.p.: Mrs. O.H. Clark, 1920.
Jno. Robertson, comp. *Michigan in the War.* Lansing, MI: W.S. George and Co. State Printers and Binders, 1882.

The Road to Freedom

Thomas, Dr. Nathan, and Pamela Thomas. *Nathan M. Thomas: Birthright Member of the Society of Friends, Pioneer Physician, Early and Earnest Advocate of the Abolition of Slavery, Friend and Helper of the Fugitive Slave.* Cassopolis, MI: Stanton B. Thomas, 1925.

Bibliography

Chapter 2

Abraham Lincoln's Visit to Kalamazoo

Kalamazoo Daily Telegraph, December 2, 1893.
Letter from Abraham Lincoln to Hezekiah G. Wells, August 4, 1856. Kalamazoo Valley Museum. https://collections.kvcc.edu.
Starr, Thomas Irwin, and Joseph J Lewis. *Lincoln's Kalamazoo Address Against Extending Slavery.* Detroit, MI: Fine Book Circle, 1941.

Chapter 3

Everts and Abbott. *History of Kalamazoo County Michigan.* Philadelphia: J.B. Lippincott Press, 1880.
Kalamazoo Daily Telegraph, May 31, 1876.
Kalamazoo Gazette. "Fireman's Hall." August 27, 1852,

Tensions Run High

Devens, Richard M. *Assault on the Hon. Charles Sumner, by Hon. Preston S. Brooks. Chicago: American Progress, 1882.*
Kalamazoo Gazette. "The Meeting at Vicksburg: How It Got Up, How Disturbed, and by Whom, What Took Place, What Resolutions Were Passed." August 30, 1861.

Chapter 4

Adjutant-General's Department and George H. Turner, *Record of Service of Michigan Volunteers in the Civil War, 1861–1865.* Vol. 2, 6, 13, 25, 44 and 46. Kalamazoo, MI: Ihiling Bros & Everard, 1905.
Everts and Abbott. *History of Kalamazoo County Michigan.* Philadelphia: J.B. Lippincott Press, 1880.
Jno. Robertson. *Michigan in the War.* Revised ed. Lansing, MI: W.S. George and Company, 1882.

Bibliography

Kalamazoo Gazette. "Red, White and Blue." April 26, 1861.
———. "Special Meeting of the Board of Supervisors." May 17, 1861.
Letter from James Nickerson, private, 11th Michigan Cavalry, to his parents, June 1864.

The Casualties Begin

Email from Lynn Houghton, March 26, 2020. Western Michigan University Archives. Humphrey Block History—Peninsula Building.
Kalamazoo Gazette, September 25, 1905.

All Roads Lead from Kalamazoo County

Adjutant-General's Department and George H. Turner, *Record of Service of Michigan Volunteers in the Civil War, 1861–1865*. Vols. 2, 6, 13, 25, 44 and 46. Kalamazoo, MI: Ihiling Bros & Everard, 1905.
Jno. Robertson. *Michigan in the War*. Revised ed. Lansing, MI: W.S. George and Company, 1882.
Roll of Honor, No. XVIII, Names of Soldiers Who Died in Defense of the American Union, Interred in National Cemeteries…and Local Cemeteries and at Military Posts in Texas, Indiana, Illinois, Ohio, Wisconsin, Michigan, Iowa and Kansas. Vol. 18. Washington, D.C.: Government Printing Office, 1868.

Chapter 5

Adjutant-General's Department and George H. Turner, *Record of Service of Michigan Volunteers in the Civil War, 1861–1865*. Vol. 13, 46. Kalamazoo, MI: Ihiling Bros & Everard, 1905.
DiConti, Lois. "1860 Federal Census, Kalamazoo County, Michigan, African American Households." AfriGeneas. http://www.afrigeneas.com.
Glazer, Sidney, ed. *Negroes in Michigan During the Civil War*. Lansing: Michigan Civil War Centennial Observance Commission, 1966.
Riverside Cemetery Records. https://www.kalamazoocity.org.
United States General Index to Pension Files, 1861–1934. https://www.familysearch.org.

Bibliography

Wolz, Robert J. *Grand Army Men: The G.A.R. and Its Male Organizations.* Key West, FL: Key West Publishing, 2014.

Lovett Hammond

Adjutant-General's Department and George H. Turner, *Record of Service of Michigan Volunteers in the Civil War, 1861–1865.* Vol. 46. Kalamazoo, MI: Ihiling Bros & Everard, 1905.
DiConti, Lois. "1860 Federal Census, Kalamazoo County, Michigan, African American Households." AfriGeneas. http://www.afrigeneas.com.
1880 Census, Kalamazoo County, Michigan. https://www.familysearch.org.
1850 Census, Marion County, Indiana. https://www.familysearch.org.
United States General Index to Pension Files, 1861–1934. https://www.familysearch.org.
United States Records of Headstones of Deceased Union Veterans, 1879–1902, https://www.familysearch.org.

Thomas Woodford

Adjutant-General's Department and George H. Turner, *Record of Service of Michigan Volunteers in the Civil War, 1861–1865.* Vol. 46. Kalamazoo, MI: Ihiling Bros & Everard, 1905.
DiConti, Lois. "1860 Federal Census, Kalamazoo County, Michigan, African American Households." AfriGeneas. http://www.afrigeneas.com.
Kalamazoo Daily Telegraph. "Town Topics." March 23, 1895.
Kalamazoo Gazette. "Among the Dead." March 24, 1895.
United States General Index to Pension Files, 1861–1934. https://www.familysearch.org.

Rix Hammond

Adjutant-General's Department and George H. Turner, *Record of Service of Michigan Volunteers in the Civil War, 1861–1865.* Vol. 32, 46. Kalamazoo, MI: Ihiling Bros & Everard, 1905.
DiConti, Lois. "1860 Federal Census, Kalamazoo County, Michigan, African American Households." AfriGeneas. http://www.afrigeneas.com.

Bibliography

Kalamazoo Daily Telegraph. "Recorder's Court—Judge Peck." November 6, 1896.
Kalamazoo Evening Telegraph. "Town Topics." May 12, 1894.
Minutes, May 15, 1894, Orcutt Post No. 79, GAR. Kalamazoo Valley Museum.
United States General Index to Pension Files, 1861–1934. https://www.familysearch.org.

Aaron Burnett

Adjutant-General's Department and George H. Turner, *Record of Service of Michigan Volunteers in the Civil War, 1861–1865*. Vol. 46. Kalamazoo, MI: Ihiling Bros & Everard, 1905.
DiConti, Lois. "1860 Federal Census, Kalamazoo County, Michigan, African American Households." AfriGeneas. http://www.afrigeneas.com.
United States General Index to Pension Files, 1861–1934. https://www.familysearch.org.

Elijah Harris

Adjutant-General's Department and George H. Turner, *Record of Service of Michigan Volunteers in the Civil War, 1861–1865*. Vol. 46. Kalamazoo, MI: Ihiling Bros & Everard, 1905.
DiConti, Lois. "1860 Federal Census, Kalamazoo County, Michigan, African American Households." AfriGeneas. http://www.afrigeneas.com.
United States General Index to Pension Files, 1861–1934. https://www.familysearch.org.

Edward Kersey

Adjutant-General's Department and George H. Turner, *Record of Service of Michigan Volunteers in the Civil War, 1861–1865*. Vol. 46. Kalamazoo, MI: Ihiling Bros & Everard, 1905.
Death Record, State of Michigan. seekingmichigan.contentdm.oclc.org.
DiConti, Lois. "1860 Federal Census, Kalamazoo County, Michigan, African American Households." AfriGeneas. http://www.afrigeneas.com.
United States General Index to Pension Files, 1861–1934. https://www.familysearch.org.

Bibliography

Stephen White

Adjutant-General's Department and George H. Turner, *Record of Service of Michigan Volunteers in the Civil War, 1861–1865*. Vol. 46. Kalamazoo, MI: Ihiling Bros & Everard, 1905.
DiConti, Lois. "1860 Federal Census, Kalamazoo County, Michigan, African American Households." AfriGeneas. http://www.afrigeneas.com.
Kalamazoo Telegraph. January 25, 1876.
———. "Jottings." January 24, 1876.
United States General Index to Pension Files, 1861–1934. https://www.familysearch.org.

Chapter 6

The Ladies' Aid Society

Cornelia R. Sheldon, Obituary. https://www.findagrave.com.
Everts and Abbott. *History of Kalamazoo County Michigan*. Philadelphia: J.B. Lippincott Press, 1880.
Kalamazoo Daily Telegraph. "Funeral of Mrs. Joseph Sill." Obituary, December 21, 1898.
———. "Was a Ministering Angel to the Boys in Blue." Mary Penfield Obituary, July 30, 1897.
Kalamazoo Evening Telegraph. "Death of Dr. Sill." Obituary, April 24, 1905.
Kalamazoo Gazette. "Death Takes Mrs. Potter at Age of 94." January 4, 1921.
Kalamazoo Saturday Telegraph. "Miss Penfield's Work." April 16, 1898.
Kalamazoo Telegraph. "Soldiers Aid Society." December 2, 1863.
Spiro, Robert. "The Ladies Behind the Men Behind the Guns: Michigan, 1861–1865." *Quarterly Review of Michigan Alumnus* 67 (Autumn 1960).
"Sudden Death." Mrs. Ruth Webster Obituary. https://www.findagrave.com.
Records of Burials, City of Kalamazoo, http://www.cemeteryregister.com.

The Draft

Adjutant-General's Department and George H. Turner, *Record of Service of Michigan Volunteers in the Civil War, 1861–1865*. Vol. 14, 15, 16, 17 and 32. Kalamazoo, MI: Ihiling Bros & Everard, 1905.

Bibliography

Everts and Abbott. *History of Kalamazoo County Michigan*. Philadelphia: J.B. Lippincott Press, 1880.
Kalamazoo Gazette. "The Draft! Call for Volunteers." October 24, 1862.
Kalamazoo Telegraph, December 2, 1863.

Chapter 7

Spontaneous, Individual Explosion

Kalamazoo Daily Telegraph. "Appomattox." Evening edition, February 10, 1894.

A Convulsive Shudder

Kalamazoo Daily Telegraph. "The Assassination." Evening edition, February 17, 1894.
Kalamazoo Gazette. "The President's Death." April 21, 1865.

For Gallantry in Action

Adjutant-General's Department and George H. Turner, *Record of Service of Michigan Volunteers in the Civil War, 1861–1865*. Vol. 36. Kalamazoo, MI: Ihiling Bros & Everard, 1905.
"Elliott Malloy Norton." https://www.findagrave.com.
Michigan Deaths and Burials, 1800–1995. Familysearch.org.
Milbrook, Minnie Dubbs. "Heroes in Washington." Chap. 3 in *A Study in Valor: Michigan Medal of Honor Winners in the Civil War*. Lansing, MI: Civil War Centennial Observance Commission, 1966.

Chapter 8

Our Very Own Rebel

Confederate Veteran. Vol. 18. Nashville, TN: N.p., 1910.

Bibliography

Field, Ron. *Tennessee & North Carolina*. Vol. 5 of *The Confederate Army 1861–65*. With illustrations by Richard Hook. Oxford, UK: Osprey Publishing, 2007.

Kalamazoo Daily Telegraph. "The Opera House." May 25, 1881,

Kalamazoo Death Records, 1916–1933. http://www.kalamazoogenealogy.org.

Kalamazoo Telegraph. "City in Brief." June 27, 1903. (The date in the database lists this issue as 1906, not 1903.)

———. "Fizz! Bang! Boom!" July 5, 1889.

———. "Tooth Too Tough." September 26, 1911.

Provemont Courier. "Death Notice." July 14, 1916. https://www.findagrave.com.

Scientific American 17, no. 26 (December 28, 1867). http://archive.org.

Specifications and Drawings of Patents Issued from the U.S. Patent Office, March 17, 1874.

Kalamazoo's Claim on Memorial Day

Adjutant-General's Department and George H. Turner, *Record of Service of Michigan Volunteers in the Civil War, 1861–1865*. Vol. 2. Kalamazoo, MI: Ihiling Bros & Everard, 1905.

Indianapolis Journal, May 31, 1902.

Kalamazoo Daily Telegraph. "Was the First to Decorate Graves at Arlington Cemetery." May 30, 1900.

National Tribune (Washington, D.C.), February 21, 1884. (The *National Tribune* was a monthly and later weekly paper published from 1877 to 1917 for Union veterans of the Civil War and their families. It was the unofficial publication of the Grand Army of the Republic.)

The Murder of Sheriff Benjamin F. Orcutt

Everts and Abbott. *History of Kalamazoo County Michigan*. Philadelphia: J.B. Lippincott Press, 1880.

Kalamazoo Daily Telegraph. "A Card from Mrs. Orcutt to the Editor of the Telegraph." November 21, 1871.

———. "The Case of Mrs. Orcutt." October 23, 1869.

———. "The Murderer of Sheriff Orcutt Arrested." February 3, 1869.

Youngs, James (former Kalamazoo county clerk), in conversation with author.

Bibliography

The Veterans Organize

Adjutant-General's Department and George H. Turner, *Record of Service of Michigan Volunteers in the Civil War, 1861–1865*. Vol. 13. Kalamazoo, MI: Ihiling Bros & Everard, 1905.

Department of Arkansas 23rd Department Encampment Proceedings, Grand Army of the Republic 1905.

Indigent Veterans of Kalamazoo County Record Book. Zang Legacy Collections Center. Western Michigan University Archives, Kalamazoo, Michigan.

Wolz, Robert J. *Grand Army Men: The GAR and Its Male Organizations*. Key West, FL: Key West Publishing, 2014.

Memorial Day

"General John A. Logan's General Order 11." Memorial Day. http://www.usmemorialday.org.

Kalamazoo Gazette. "Honoring the Dead." June 8, 1888. Collection of Michael Culp.

Orcutt Post No. 79

Grand Army of the Republic Ritual. Philadelphia: Burk & McFetridge Printers, 1888.

Honor Roll of Kalamazoo County. N.p.: Mrs. O.H. Clark, 1920.

Kalamazoo Gazette, February 20, 1885. Collection of Michael Culp.

Kalamazoo Telegraph. "Heroes of '61." September 23, 1901.

Quarterly Reports, Orcutt Post No. 79, Grand Army of the Republic. 1882. Michigan History Center Archives *Records of Posts, Michigan GAR, 1876–1945*. Records of the Grand Army of the Republic, Department of Michigan. 81 boxes. RG 63-19.

The description of the water fountain in the GAR Hall being plumbed through a canteen was part of a presentation at the Vicksburg Historical Society in 2011, by Art O'Leary of Portage, Michigan.

Bibliography

Orcutt Corps No. 110, Woman's Relief Corps

Records of the Department of Michigan, Woman's Relief Corps, Auxiliary to the Grand Army of the Republic. Grand Army of the Republic Memorial Hall & Museum, Eaton Rapids, Michigan.

Other Posts Organized in Kalamazoo County

Journals of the Annual Encampment, Department of Michigan Grand Army of the Republic. Department of Michigan, Grand Army of the Republic. Proceedings of 1887, 1890, 1905–1907, 1909, 1910, 1912–1919, 1921–1940, 1942–1948. Hathi Trust. https://catalog.hathitrust.org.

Kalamazoo Gazette. "Veterans Falling Fast Before Reaper." May 30, 1909. Collection of Michael Culp.

The Last Man

The story of Smith Carlton obstructing the razing of the GAR Hall has been circulating in the Kalamazoo area for at least forty years. The original source has yet to be determined but seems plausible.

Monuments of Kalamazoo

Kalamazoo Evening Telegraph. "Mrs. Mary Osborn Gives Monument." June 1, 1909.

Orcutt Post Lot

Honor Roll of Kalamazoo County. N.p.: Mrs. O.H. Clark, 1920.
Kalamazoo Daily Telegraph. "Dedication of Soldiers' Lot." May 31, 1888.
———. "The Patriots' Shrine." June 1, 1888.

Bibliography

Chapter 9

George K. Shannon

Adjutant-General's Department and George H. Turner, *Record of Service of Michigan Volunteers in the Civil War, 1861–1865*. Vol. 2. Kalamazoo, MI: Ihiling Bros & Everard, 1905.

Kalamazoo Evening Telegraph. "Flag Wrapped, Body of George Shannon Laid to Rest." January 10, 1906.

———. "George Shannon, Veteran Hack Driver Dies in Borgess Hospital Today." January 8, 1906.

———. "Shannon Was Brave Soldier, On Battlefield He Remembered His Comrade, Orderly Shakespeare Was First, When Wounded Carried Off the Field." January 13, 1906.

John Bigham

Adjutant-General's Department and George H. Turner, *Record of Service of Michigan Volunteers in the Civil War, 1861–1865*. Vol. 13. Kalamazoo, MI: Ihiling Bros & Everard, 1905.

Kalamazoo Gazette. "Comstock: John Bigham's Record." August 19, 1890.

———. "Comstock Clatter." April 19, 1894.

———. "Comstock Clatter." May 2, 1894.

———. "Comstock Clatter: An Interesting Letter From the 'Zoo's Suburb." May 2, 1894.

———. "A Fraudulent Pensioner." August 16, 1890.

Pension Certificate, December 29, 1892. United States General Index to Pension Files. familysearch.org.

Ellis McGerry

"Company Descriptive Book, 55th (Col'd.) Mass." fold3.com.

Kalamazoo Evening Telegraph. "M'Gerry Dies Amid Vermin, Was Ex-Slave and Union Army Man." January 1, 1907.

———. "Not A G.A.R. Member. Members of Orcutt Post Know Nothing About McGerry." January 2, 1907.

———. "Two Colored Men Who Fought in the Civil War Living in Kalamazoo." August 1, 1901.

BIBLIOGRAPHY

Kalamazoo Gazette. "Slave-Soldier Dies in a Hovel, Aged Colored Man Found Dead Yesterday Morning in North Street Ally." January 2, 1907.

Ira H. Curtiss

Kalamazoo Gazette. "Don't Want His Money, Mrs. Ira Curtiss Thinks Her Husband Was Killed." September 15, 1895.
———. "Suddenly Insane, the Asylum Meat Cutter Suicides. Slashed His Throat." September 12, 1895.
Michigan Marriages, 1822–1995. familysearch.org.
Muster Rolls of the U.S.S. *Maratanza*, 1862–65. National Archives, Washington, D.C.
Pension File, (10 pages) Pension Records. fold3.com.
United States Census, Muskegon, Muskegon County, Michigan, 1880. familysearch.org.

Stanley B. Cowing

Kalamazoo Gazette. "Devoted Couple Go to Grave Together after 10-Year Tryst Since Wife Died." March 20, 1921.
Morris, Peter, William J. Ryczek and Jan Finkel. *Base Ball Pioneers, 1850–1870: The Clubs and Players Who Spread the Sport Nationwide.* Jefferson, NC: McFarland Books, 2012.
Records of the Michigan Soldiers' Home, Register No. 6875. Microfilm. Grand Rapids Public Library.
Record, 2nd Mounted Rifles New York State Military Museum Unit History Project. https://dmna.ny.gov.
"Stanley Cowing Played Semi-Professional Baseball for the Buffalo Niagara's from 1865 to 1868." Threads of Our Game. https://www.threadsofourgame.com.
"Steve Riddle's Family Tree." RootsWeb World Connect. http://wc.rootsweb.com.

Benjamin F. Stewart

Company Descriptive Book, 15th Infantry USCT. fold3.com.

Bibliography

"Return of Deaths, Kalamazoo County, Michigan, for the Month of January 1918." https://www.familysearch.org.

United States Census Household Record, Newburg, Cass County, Michigan, 1880. http://www.familysearch.org.

United States Veterans Administration Pension Payment Cards, 1907–1933. https://www.familysearch.org.

Henry O. Barker

"Declaration for an Original Invalid Pension." Pension Records. fold3.com.

Kalamazoo Gazette. "Among the Dead." September 19, 1895.

Records of the Michigan Soldiers' Home, Register No. 1536. Microfilm. Grand Rapids Public Library.

Edward S. Taylor

Adjutant-General's Department and George H. Turner, *Record of Service of Michigan Volunteers in the Civil War, 1861–1865*. Vol. 44. Kalamazoo, MI: Ihiling Bros & Everard, 1905.

Kalamazoo Gazette. "Jottings, Obituary." March 24, 1892.

Kalamazoo Telegraph. "An Old Soldier's Body Saved from the Dissecting Knives of Ann Arbor Medical Students." March 23, 1892.

Michigan Marriages 1822–1995. https://www.familysearch.org.

Arthur d'Armand

Dibean, Jack and Marianne Dibean. "Branch County, Michigan Dibean Marriage Index." MIGenWeb Archives. March 2014. http://files.usgwarchives.net.

Kalamazoo College Bulletin 2, no. 2 (1907). https://cache.kzoo.edu.

Kalamazoo Daily Telegraph. "French Academy." September 20, 1875.

———. "Garlands on the Grave, Ceremony Beautifully Carried Out This Morning." May 30, 1900.

———. "Laid to Rest." January 12, 1887.

———. "Prof. D'Armand Dying." January 8, 1887.

Bibliography

Michigan Department of Public Instruction. *Annual Report of the Superintendent of Public Instruction of the State of Michigan.* N.p: W.S. George & Co., State Printers, 1876.

Cyrus S. Welch

Adjutant-General's Department and George H. Turner, *Record of Service of Michigan Volunteers in the Civil War, 1861–1865.* Vol. 13, 36. Kalamazoo, MI: Ihiling Bros & Everard, 1905.
Jackson Daily Citizen. "Peninsular Paragraphs. Brief Items of Interest Gathered from All Over the State of Michigan." February 4, 1892.
Kalamazoo Gazette. "Jottings." February 3, 1892.
———. "Tuesday." August 2, 1889.
Michael B. Culp, transcriber. "13th Michigan Infantry Descriptive Book." 2013. National Archives, Washington, D.C.
Records of the Michigan Soldiers' Home, Register No. 1026. Microfilm. Grand Rapids Public Library.

Ezra S. Scott

Adjutant-General's Department and George H. Turner, *Record of Service of Michigan Volunteers in the Civil War, 1861–1865.* Vols. 4, 44. Kalamazoo, MI: Ihiling Bros & Everard, 1905.
"Grand Army of the Republic Records Project, Individual Record, Post 35." Sons of Union Veterans of the Civil War. suvcwmi.org.
Herek, Raymond J. *These Men Have Seen Hard Service: The First Michigan Sharpshooters in the Civil War* Detroit, MI: Wayne State University Press, 1998.
Kalamazoo Gazette. "Funeral of Ezra Scott." September 26, 1905.
"Wheeler and Many Allied Families." Rootsweb World Connect Project. wc.rootsweb.ancestory.com.

Thomas W. Warren

Adjutant-General's Department and George H. Turner, *Record of Service of Michigan Volunteers in the Civil War, 1861–1865.* Vol. 19. Kalamazoo, MI: Ihiling Bros & Everard, 1905.

Bibliography

Kalamazoo Evening News. "In Prosecutors Hands. Detective Warren Has Placed Testimony in Schilling Murder Case." January 27, 1899.

Kalamazoo Evening Telegraph. "Keep No Sleuth. Doesn't Appeal to Officers. Say They Have Investigated His Story That Brother William Was Guilty of Murdering Schilling." August 3, 1909.

Kalamazoo Gazette. "Common Council, Reports." October 10, 1884.

———. "Common Council, Reports." October 14, 1884.

———. "Had a Lively Time: A Crazy Man Outruns Detective Thomas Warren." June 12, 1894.

———. "The Man in the Moon: The Social Evil and the Causes Talked Over Plainly." August 7, 1887.

———. "Special Meeting City Council." October 24, 1884.

———. "Thomas Warren Drops Dead Tuesday." September 12, 1906.

William Hawthorne

Adjutant-General's Department and George H. Turner, *Record of Service of Michigan Volunteers in the Civil War, 1861–1865*. Vol. 2. Kalamazoo, MI: Ihling Bros & Everard, 1905.

Kalamazoo Telegraph. "Obituary. William Hawthorne." December 28, 1901.

Records of the Michigan Soldiers' Home, Register No. 1144. Microfilm. Grand Rapids Public Library.

United States Census Household Record, Kalamazoo County, Michigan, 1900. http://www.familysearch.org.

The letters of the Hodgman Family can be found in the Western Michigan University Archives, Hodgman Letters, 1852–1862. Davis and Temple Collection, A-180.

Index

Numerals

1st Michigan Cavalry 30, 75, 96, 130, 142, 144, 145, 146, 147, 148, 149, 150, 151
1st Michigan Colored Infantry 53, 55, 57, 93, 142, 146, 149
1st Michigan Sharpshooters 46, 49, 90, 126, 127, 132, 143, 145, 148, 149, 150, 152
5th Michigan Cavalry 30, 100, 130, 142, 143, 144, 145, 147, 148, 149, 151, 152
6th Michigan Infantry/Artillery 10, 33, 34, 35, 46, 74, 90, 142, 143, 144, 145, 146, 147, 149, 150, 152
11th Michigan Cavalry 43, 44, 90, 106, 142, 143, 144, 145, 146, 147, 150, 152
13th Michigan Infantry 27, 36, 39, 46, 68, 90, 96, 99, 110, 118, 129, 142, 143, 144, 145, 146, 147, 148, 149, 150, 151, 152
14th Battery 46
17th Michigan Infantry 30, 68, 90, 142, 143, 145, 146, 148, 149, 150, 151
18th United States Infantry 30
25th Michigan Infantry 39, 41, 42, 80, 142, 143, 144, 145, 146, 147, 148, 149, 150, 151
28th Michigan Infantry 42, 102, 145, 148, 150, 151
102nd United States Colored Troops 55, 56, 59, 60, 67, 68, 93, 119

A

Acker Corps No. 176 97
Acker Post No. 220 96, 97
Alexander Morgan 60
Andersonville 49, 110, 115
Ann Arbor, Michigan 13, 54, 127
Arcadia Creek 9
Ash, Ashberry 59

Index

B

Baldwin, Florida 55
Bannister, Dr. Burr 76, 77
Bannister, Guy 77
Bannister, Lucy 77
Bannister, Walter 77
Barker, Henry O. 125, 126
Barnes, Henry 52, 53
Bass, James H. 59, 93
Baton Rouge, Louisiana 35
Battle Creek, Michigan 12, 13, 52, 53, 126, 127
Baxter, Charlotte Ann 50
Beauregard, Nathan 59, 93
Bennett, Edward L. 59
Bentonville, North Carolina 36
Bigham, John 117, 118
Blackburn's Ford, Virginia 32, 113
Blair, Austin 28, 29, 43, 53, 54, 63
Blair Guard 29
Boykin, South Carolina 55
Breese, John W. 25
Bristol, Tennessee 44
Bronson Park 14, 15, 21, 22, 34, 72, 80, 104, 106
Brown, Simeon B. 43
Bruce, J.W. 23
Burdick House Hotel 15, 30
Burnett, Aaron 57
Burnside, General Ambrose E. 55, 62, 132
Burson, Abner H. 100, 144
Burson, Joseph 100, 144
Burson, Milton 100
Burson Post No. 303 100, 102
Burson, Warren 100

C

Calloway, Creed 59
Camp Barry, D.C. 46
Camp Ward 53
Carlton, Smith H. 102, 104
Carpenter's Corners 10
Carrier, Henry B. 143
Cass County, Michigan 12, 53, 124
Cassopolis, Michigan 55
Chattanooga, Tennessee 36, 99
Chickamauga, Georgia 36, 99
Church, Harry C. 32
Climax, Michigan 5, 10, 13, 23, 28, 63, 67, 71, 99, 139
Cobb, Thomas 25
Cooper, Michigan 10, 75
Cowing, Stanley B. 122, 123
Cuckwold's Creek Bridge 55
Curtenius, Frederick 23, 25, 33, 80, 90
Curtiss, Ira H. 120, 121
Cynthia, Kentucky 44, 96

D

d'Armand, Arthur 128
Daughters of Union Veterans of the Civil War 21
Davis, E.H. 25
Dearborn, Michigan 46, 47, 126, 132
DeLand, Charles V. 46, 47, 49
Democratic Party 20
Detroit, Michigan 6, 9, 13, 32, 33, 42, 52, 53, 55, 56, 57, 59, 63, 84, 115, 131, 132, 133, 136
Deveaux Neck, South Carolina 55, 59, 119

Index

Dooling, Reverend 52
Dudgeon, John 25

E

Early, Jubal 46
Edmunds, Sarah. *See* Thompson, Franklin
Eugene H. Bronson Post No. 295 99
Evans, George 79
Evans, Sarah 78, 79

F

Fireman's Hall 23
First Bull Run (Manassas) 32
Fisher, David A. 25
Fort Bunker Hill 46
Fort Slemmer 46
Fort Steadman 49
Fort Stevens 5, 23, 46, 79, 113, 137
Fort Totton 46
Fort Wayne 5, 32
Fredericksburg, Virginia 32, 78, 79, 114
Freeland, John. *See* Whaling, Albert
Freeman, Benjamin 49, 145
Fulton, Michigan 10, 96

G

Galesburg, Michigan 10, 71, 99, 139
Giddings, Dr. Marsh 25
G.L. Hudson Post No. 317 102

Grahmsville, South Carolina 55
Grand Review 33, 36, 49, 127
Grand Traverse, Michigan 46
Grant, General Ulysses S. 55, 62, 71, 76, 86, 129
Green, George F. 77

H

Hackley, Calvin 59
Hammond, Benjamin 56
Hammond, Lovett 56, 57, 59
Hammond, Mary 56, 59
Hammond, Rebecca 56
Hammond, Rix 56, 57, 59, 65, 67, 68
Harris, Elijah 57, 60, 146
Hartsuff, Major General 41
Hatcher's Run 32, 127
Hawthorne, William 136
Hedges, Spencer 60
Henderson, George 60
Henderson, Samuel 60, 93
Hodgman, Frances 139
Hodgman, Frank 61, 139
Hodgman, Moses 5, 28, 52
Hodgman, Samuel 23, 139
Honey Hill, South Carolina 55, 119
Humphrey Block 28, 30
Hussey, Erastus 12, 13
Hyatt, Jennings 60

J

Jackson, James 60

Index

Jackson, Michigan 15, 36, 44, 46, 49, 54, 62, 107
Jackson, Mississippi 32, 114

K

Kalamazoo Light Guard 28, 91
Kalamazoo River 9, 50, 93
Kellogg, Israel 23
Kersey, Edward 57, 59, 60
Kersey, Sophia (Bolden) 59
Kingston, North Carolina 42
Knoxville, Tennessee 32, 114

L

Ladies' Aid Society 61, 63, 64, 86
Ladies' Library Association 63, 64, 65
Lelanau, Michigan 46
Lemon, Theodore 50, 147
Lenoir Station 32
Lexington, Kentucky 44
Lincoln, Abraham 5, 14, 15, 21, 23, 24, 26, 27, 62, 70, 72, 73, 79, 83, 100, 137
Logan, John A. 87, 88, 90
Lookout Mountain, Tennessee 36

M

Mallory, George 60
Malvern Hill 32
March to the Sea 36, 102
Marshall, Michigan 13, 42, 55
Mattawan, Michigan 102

May, Charles S. 28, 32, 70, 71, 72, 136
May, Dwight 23, 25, 32, 55, 78, 89
May, Ella 78, 79
May, Josephine 78, 79
May, Maria 78, 79
May, Reverend Franklin W. 78
McCullough, Achillies 60
McGerry, Ellis 60, 119
McNair, Dr. Rush 77
Memorial Day 78, 79, 85, 87, 88, 89, 93, 94, 112, 141
Michigan Soldiers' Home 110, 126, 131
Miller, Joseph 25
Mission Ridge, Tennessee 36
Moffat, General Isaac 23
Montague, Captain Calvin 55
Moore, Colonel Orlando H. 39, 40, 41, 42, 107
Morgan, General John 39, 40, 42
Morgan, George 60
Morgan, John Hunt 44, 47, 49, 132
Mottram, William 25
Mountain Home Cemetery 31, 63, 64, 77, 79, 82
Mount Sterling, Kentucky 44

N

Nashville, Tennessee 36, 42, 44, 99, 124
National Driving Park 29
North Anna, Virginia 32, 127
Norton, Abbie 75
Norton, Effie 75
Norton, Elliott 74, 75
Norton, Lucy 75

Index

Norton, Max 75
Norvell, John M. 32

O

Orcutt, Benjamin 28, 80, 81, 83, 89, 94, 107
Orcutt Post No. 79 56, 60, 89, 90, 91, 93, 99, 102, 104, 107, 110, 112, 113, 117, 137

P

Park, George W. 32
Perrin, L.W. 30
Perry, Oliver H. 30
Perryville, Kentucky 36, 111
Portage Center, Michigan 10
Porter, Captain Thomas K. 76
Port Hudson, Alabama 35
Potter, Allen 64
Potter, Charity 64
Potter, Ruth 61
Prairie Rhonde 11, 67
Pratt, Dr. Foster 26, 27, 36
Pulaski, Tennessee 44

R

Republican Party 14, 15, 23
Riverside Cemetery 11, 50, 56, 57, 59, 60, 107, 112, 115, 117, 118, 119, 127, 129, 141
Roanoke, Virginia 44
Robbins, Reuben 60, 93
Robbins, Simeon 60, 93, 119

Roberts, William H. 60, 93
Robinson, William Riley 60

S

Salisbury, North Carolina 44, 107, 136
Saltville, Virginia 44
Savannah, Georgia 36, 102
Schoolcraft Cemetery 13, 100
Schoolcraft, Michigan 9, 10, 11, 13, 23, 26, 39, 44, 71, 75, 97, 100, 135
Scott, Ezra 132
Scott, Ezra S. 131
Scott, Lucy M. 94
Scott, Preston 60
Scotts, Michigan 10, 99, 100
Seymour, Indiana 47, 49
Shakespeare, William 29, 107, 110, 113, 117, 127
Shannon, George K. 113, 115, 117
Sheldon, Cornelia Stockbridge 61, 63
Sheldon, Theodore Pierce 63
Sheppard, Edward 60
Shoemaker, Michael 36
Shutgart, Zachariah 12
Siege of Corinth, Mississippi 36
Siege of Mobile, Alabama 35
Siege of Petersburg, Virginia 32, 127
Simmons, Charles 60
Simmons, William Henry 60
Singleton's plantation, South Carolina 55
Skipworth, Richard 60
Sons of Union Veterans of the Civil War 7, 8, 104, 107, 110

Spotsylvania, Virginia 32
Spring Hill, South Carolina 55
Stanton, Edwin M. 53
Stewart, Benjamin F. 124
Stoddart, William H. 77
Stone, Lucinda Hinsdale 61
Stone's River, Tennessee 36
Sumterville, South Carolina 55
Swift Creek, South Carolina 55

T

Taylor, Edward 126
Taylor, Frank 50, 150
Tebb's Bend, Kentucky 39, 42
Thomas, Dr. Nathan M. 11, 12, 13
Thomas, Pamela 11, 12, 13
Tillifinny, South Carolina 55
Tillman, Harrison H. 60

U

Underground Railroad 12
unknowns 51

V

Vicksburg, Michigan 10, 11, 12, 26, 96
Vicksburg, Mississippi 32, 35

W

Walbridge, Samuel 23, 25
Walker, Sanger and Edwards 30

Walter Orr Post No. 312 99, 100
Warren, Thomas W. 133, 134, 135
Washington, D.C. 32, 33, 36, 46, 49, 50, 53, 72, 73, 75, 78, 79, 87, 118, 127, 129, 130, 131, 136
Washington Square 11, 29, 42
Webster, David 63
Webster, Ruth 61, 63
Welch, Cyrus S. 129, 130, 131
Weldon Railroad 32, 49
Wells, Hezekiah G. 14, 15, 23, 25, 36
Whaling, Albert 60
White, Henry 59
White, Jennie 59
White Oak Swamp 32, 114
White, Stephen 59, 60
White, William 59
Wilderness, Virginia 32, 49, 127, 130, 132
Wilson, Gilbert 25
Winslow, George Washington 15, 26
Woodbury, James P. 25
Woodford, Thomas 56, 59, 60, 93
Wyse Forks, North Carolina 42

Y

Yorkville, Michigan 10

About the Author

Gary L. Gibson is a lifelong resident of the Kalamazoo area. A graduate of Kalamazoo Valley Community College (KVCC) and Western Michigan University, he formerly worked in the archives of KVCC. He is currently the curator of exhibits of Michigan's Grand Army of the Republic Memorial Hall and Museum and serves as the secretary on its board of directors. Gary is a companion of the Military Order of the Loyal Legion of the United States, past commander of the Department of Michigan, Sons of Union Veterans of the Civil War and past president of the Sons of the Revolution in the State of Michigan. Gary resides in Cooper Township with his best friend and wife of twenty-eight years, Beth.

Visit us at
www.historypress.com